fab food

retro classics

Published by Murdoch Books®, a division of Murdoch Magazines Pty Ltd.

Murdoch Books® Australia
GPO Box 1203
Sydney NSW 1045
Phone: + 61 (0) 2 4352 7000
Fax: + 61 (0) 2 4352 7026

Murdoch Books UK Limited
Ferry House
51–57 Lacy Road
Putney, London SW15 1PR
Phone: + 44 (0) 20 8355 1480
Fax: + 44 (0) 20 8355 1499

Design Concept: Marylouise Brammer
Designer: Susanne Geppert
Recipe introductions: Lucy Campbell
Editorial Director: Diana Hill
Editor: Zoë Harpham
Food Director: Lulu Grimes
Recipes developed by the Murdoch Books Test Kitchen.

Chief Executive: Juliet Rogers
Publisher: Kay Scarlett
Production Manager: Kylie Kirkwood

National Library of Australia Cataloguing-in-Publication Data
Fab food. Includes index. ISBN 1 74045 192 9. 1. Cookery. 641.5.

PRINTED IN CHINA by Toppan Printing Co. (HK) Ltd.
Printed 2002.

IMPORTANT: Those who might be at risk from the effects of salmonella food poisoning (the elderly, pregnant women, young children and those suffering from immune deficiency diseases) should consult their GP with any concerns about eating raw eggs.

fab food
retro classics

MURDOCH
BOOKS

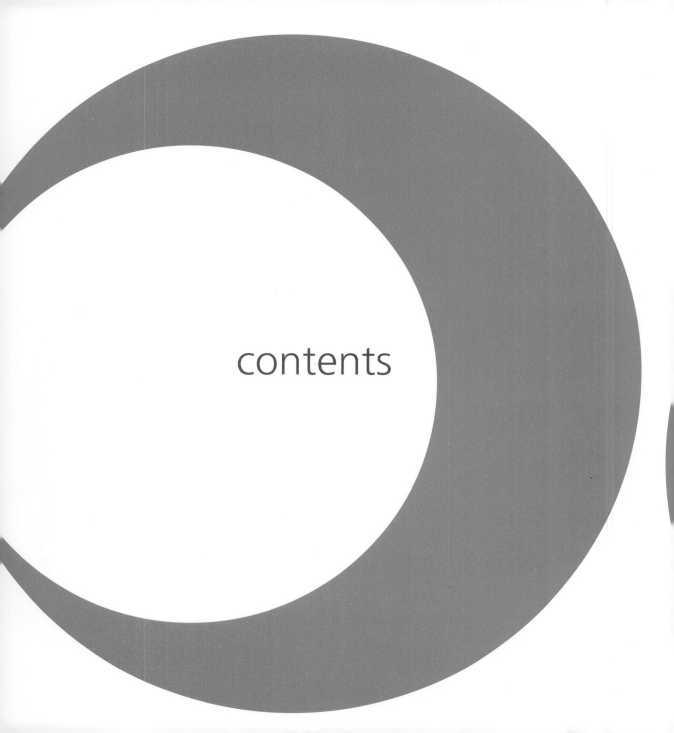

contents

from fondue to fajitas   6

party bites   8

for starters   40

the main event   60

something on the side   150

midnight suppers   172

sweet satisfaction   194

tea time   226

index   252

from fondue to fajitas

There are many things that are essential for survival, but only two things that are crucial to the good life: food and fashion. The relationship between them dictates what we eat and where we eat. Food we thought was firmly rooted in the seventies is back in vogue — before you know it you'll be sitting down to feast on chicken Kiev or beef Wellington and wondering how you ever lived without them. The trend of dinner-time retro boils down to just a couple of important ingredients: fresh food that's flavoured with a sense of fun. While guests no doubt appreciate the trouble you take all day in the kitchen preparing a three-course five-star meal, it's actually just as enjoyable for everyone if you bring out the fondue set, open the wine and settle in for a cheese or chocolate dip-a-thon.

With that in mind, this book is composed of favourite recipes from the past, dishes that at some stage were all the rage. Specialities like lobster mornay, steak Diane and baked Alaska that once graced the menu of every good restaurant in town, have come full circle to relive their glory days. Retro is hip again, influencing our tastes not only in food, but also in fashion, music and décor. It's time to take a good look at what we've left behind, and have a little fun in the kitchen again. So go with the flow and use these recipes to indulge in a little culinary grooving.

party bites

Pick an angelic oyster or, for something more sinful, let yourself be tempted by one of the dark and devilish prunes.

angels and devils on horseback

8 bacon rashers, each rasher
cut into 3 pieces
12 pitted prunes
12 oysters
2 tbs Worcestershire sauce
Tabasco sauce

Bamboo skewers have a tendency to catch fire, so start by soaking them in water for half an hour — you'll need 24. Wrap a portion of bacon around each prune and spear with a skewer.

Lightly sprinkle the oysters with Worcestershire sauce and some ground black pepper. Wrap each oyster in a blanket of bacon, securing with a skewer as before.

Cook under a preheated grill (broiler) or on the lightly oiled, outer edge of a barbecue flatplate until the bacon is delectably crisp, turning occasionally. Serve warm, sprinkled with a dash of Tabasco sauce to spice things up.
Makes 24.

smoked trout pâté

250 g (9 oz) smoked trout,
skinned and boned
125 g (4½ oz) butter, softened
125 g (4½ oz) cream cheese,
softened
1 tbs lemon juice
1 tsp horseradish cream
3 tbs chopped parsley
3 tbs chopped chives
toasted brown bread

Put the trout, butter and cream cheese in a food processor and blitz for about 20 seconds until you have a smooth, pastel mixture. Add the lemon juice, horseradish, parsley and chives and blitz for another 10 seconds. Taste a little of the mixture and add a touch more lemon juice if you think it needs it. Season with a little salt and pepper, then transfer to a small serving dish. Serve with hot toast. Makes 2 cups.

This pâté is best eaten fresh, but it can be refrigerated for up to four days if necessary. It's so quick to make, you should easily be able to whip it up on the day.

Fancy something a little fishy? Then dive right into this favourite from the ocean — one bite and you're hooked.

taramasalata

4 slices of white bread, crusts removed
3 tbs milk
100 g (3¹/2 oz) tarama (grey mullet roe)
1 egg yolk
1 garlic clove, crushed
1 tbs grated onion
125 ml (¹/2 cup) olive oil
4 tbs lemon juice

Soak the bread in milk for 5 minutes, then squeeze out the excess milk.

Put the tarama and egg yolk in a food processor and blitz for 10 seconds until it just comes together. Add the soggy bread, garlic and onion to the food processor and process until you have a smooth, creamy mixture — this won't take long at all. With the motor running, gradually pour in the olive oil in a thin stream — you'll definitely want to use the feed tube for this to avoid a messy accident. Keep processing until all the oil has been absorbed. Add the lemon juice a little at a time, tasting until the flavour is right.

Scoop the taramasalata into a small serving bowl or, if you're feeling artistic, pipe spirals into small pastry cases or mushroom caps for that special party appeal.
Makes 1¹/2 cups.

cheese straws

1 sheet of puff pastry
beaten egg
3 tbs finely grated Parmesan cheese

Lay the pastry on a bench and, when it has thawed, lightly brush it with egg. Cut the pastry into strips about 1.5 cm (5/8 inch) wide. Holding both ends of a strip, twist it twice in opposite directions as if you were wringing out a tea towel (but considerably more gently). Lay the twist on a lightly greased baking tray, then repeat with the rest of the pastry strips.

Sprinkle the cheese over the flat part of the twists. Bake in a 210°C (415°F/Gas 6–7) oven for 10 minutes until gorgeously golden and puffed up.
Makes 16.

Simple to make, delicious to eat and perfect for those who like to nibble when they twist.

Best eaten with a hearty appetite and washed down with a pint of lager. Guaranteed to curry favour with hungry guests.

onion bhajis with spicy sauce

For the spicy sauce:
2–3 red chillies, chopped
1 red capsicum (pepper), seeded and diced
425 g (15 oz) can chopped tomatoes
2 garlic cloves, finely chopped
2 tbs soft brown sugar
1¹/2 tbs cider vinegar

For the bhajis:
125 g (1 cup) plain (all-purpose) flour
2 tsp baking powder
1 tsp ground cumin
¹/2 tsp chilli powder
¹/2 tsp ground turmeric
2 eggs, beaten
4 onions, very thinly sliced
half a bunch of coriander (cilantro),
leaves chopped
oil, for deep-frying

Spice things up a bit with this sauce. Combine all the sauce ingredients in a saucepan and add 3 tablespoons water. Bring up to the boil, then reduce the heat to a simmer for about 20 minutes, until you have a thick, rich sauce. Take the pan off the heat, then add a good dash of salt and pepper.

To make the bhajis, sift the flour, baking powder, cumin, chilli powder, turmeric and 1 teaspoon salt into a bowl and make a well in the centre. Gradually add the combined egg and 3 tablespoons water, whisking to make a smooth lump-free batter. Stir in the onion and chopped coriander.

Deep-fry rough balls of batter, about the size of a golf ball, in batches for about 1¹/2 minutes each side, or until crispy and golden. Drain on crumpled paper towels. Serve on a platter with the spicy sauce for some dunking.
Makes about 25.

spicy koftas with cooling yoghurt dip

For the spicy koftas:
500 g (1 lb 2 oz) minced (ground) lamb
1 small onion, finely chopped
1 garlic clove, crushed
1 tbs chopped mint
1 tbs chopped coriander (cilantro)
1 tsp tomato paste (purée)
1 tsp ground cumin
1 tsp ground coriander
1/2 tsp finely chopped red chilli
1/4 tsp ground cinnamon
oil, for frying

For the cooling yoghurt dip:
1 small tomato, peeled, seeded
and finely chopped
half a Lebanese (short) cucumber,
peeled and finely chopped
1 garlic clove, crushed
1 tbs chopped mint
125 g (1/2 cup) plain yoghurt

Combine the lamb, onion, garlic, mint, chopped coriander, tomato paste, cumin, ground coriander, chilli and cinnamon in a large bowl. Get in there with your hands and mix it all together. Add a bit of salt and pepper, then roll the mixture into small balls that are about the size of a walnut.

Heat a little oil in a large heavy-based frying pan over medium heat. Cook the koftas in batches until they are nicely browned all over and have cooked through to the middle. Drain on crumpled paper towels.

The dip is very easy — simply mix all the ingredients together in a small bowl.

Skewer each kofta with a cocktail stick (the ones with cellophane on the ends are pretty special) and serve with the dip.
Makes 45.

Some like it hot but others want to play it cool, so serve these tasty meatballs with a refreshing yoghurt dip on the side.

These evocatively named little bites of bliss are delicately spiked for added pleasure. Great for a wild night in.

porcupine balls

For the porcupine balls:
220 g (1 cup) short-grain rice
5 dried Chinese mushrooms
250 g (9 oz) minced (ground) beef
250 g (9 oz) minced (ground) pork
60 g (2¼ oz) finely chopped water chestnuts
4 spring onions (scallions), finely chopped
1–2 garlic cloves, crushed
1 tsp grated fresh ginger
1 tbs soy sauce
1 egg, lightly beaten

For the dipping sauce:
3 tbs light soy sauce
2 tbs soft brown sugar
2 tbs grated fresh ginger

The first step with these spiky snacks is to soak the rice in a big bowl of cold water for at least 2 hours, then drain and spread it out to dry on paper towels.

The mushrooms also need to be soaked (in boiling water), but for much less time, only 20 minutes. Squeeze out the water, then throw away the stems and finely chop the caps. Put the chopped flesh in a large bowl with the beef, pork, water chestnuts, spring onion, garlic, ginger, soy sauce, egg and ½ teaspoon salt. Mix it up with your hands.

Divide the mixture into 24 small balls — you'll find this easier if you use wet hands. Roll each ball in rice. Put the balls in a lined bamboo steamer, leaving room for the rice to swell (depending what size steamer you have, you might need to cook these in batches). Sit the steamer over a wok half-filled with boiling water and steam for 30 minutes, or until the rice and meatballs are cooked. If the water evaporates too quickly, simply replenish with a little more boiling water.

To make the dipping sauce, mix the ingredients with 3 tablespoons water. Serve in a small bowl alongside the Porcupine balls. Makes 24.

fried whitebait

500 g (1 lb 2 oz) whitebait
4 tbs plain (all-purpose) flour
3 tbs cornflour (cornstarch)
2 tsp finely chopped parsley
oil, for deep-frying
lemon wedges

Before the whitebait are covered in flour, drain them well, then pat them dry, otherwise the flour will form clumps of dough.

Sift the flours into a bowl, stir in the parsley then season generously with salt and freshly ground pepper.

The whitebait need to be tossed in the flour mixture before you deep-fry them. The best way to do this is to take about a third of the fish, coat them and then straight away toss them in the hot oil. Cook them until crisp, but still quite pale — this will take less than 2 minutes. Remove them with a slotted spoon to a large plate lined with crumpled paper towels where they can drain. Repeat the whole process with the remaining whitebait.

Reheat the oil and fry the whitebait a second time in three batches for 1 minute each, or until lightly browned. Drain on crumpled paper towels and then serve hot with some lemon wedges.
Serves 6–8.

It's amazing what a simple batter can do to elevate an ordinary fish into the ranks of the superb. You'll never want to use this tiny tender fish as bait again.

Hot, crunchy and very moreish, these chillies are an ideal snack when you feel like playing with fire. Serve with bottles of Mexican beer with a wedge of lime in the neck.

chillies rellenos

2 x 325 g (11 1/2 oz) jars mild whole chillies
125 g (1 cup) grated Cheddar cheese
200 g (7 oz) cream cheese, softened
85 g (2/3 cup) plain (all-purpose) flour
4 eggs, lightly beaten
185 g (1 1/4 cups) cornmeal
125 g (1 1/4 cups) dry breadcrumbs
oil, for deep-frying
sour cream

Pick 24 handsome chillies about the same size. Drain them well and pat dry with paper towels. With a sharp knife, cut a slit down the length of one side of each chilli, then scrape out the seeds and membrane.

Combine the Cheddar and cream cheese and spoon a little of this cheesy mash into each chilli. Toss the chillies in flour, then egg and, finally, the combined cornmeal and breadcrumbs, which should stick to the egg in a thick layer. Now chill for 1 hour. After the hour is up, re-dip the chillies in the egg and re-roll in breadcrumbs, then cool them in the fridge for another hour.

Deep-fry the chillies in small batches until golden brown. Drain on crumpled paper towels. Serve with sour cream.
Makes 24.

hush puppies

150 g (1 cup) fine cornmeal
60 g (1/2 cup) self-raising flour
2 tbs cornflour (cornstarch)
1 tbs baking powder
1 tsp Cajun spices
1/2 tsp onion salt
1/4 tsp chilli powder
1 garlic clove, finely chopped
2 tbs grated onion
2 eggs, lightly beaten
185 ml (3/4 cup) milk
1 tbs lard
oil, for deep-frying

First of all, combine the cornmeal, flour, cornflour, baking powder, Cajun spices, onion salt and chilli powder. Next add the garlic, grated onion and beaten eggs and give a good stir to mix it all together.

Pour the milk into a small saucepan, then add the lard. Put the lid on, then pop the pan on the hob over low heat until the lard melts and the mixture is warm. Pour this over the dry mixture, then stir well. Now leave to cool.

Once the batter is cool, deep-fry tablespoons of it in small batches until they become puffy and lightly golden, turning each one a couple of times so that they cook evenly. The secret to removing them from the oil without bringing the oil with you is to use a slotted spoon or strainer. Drain on crumpled paper towels, then serve hot with a pile of serviettes (napkins).
Makes about 30.

So called because of the practice of tossing leftovers to quieten barking dogs. We suggest you avoid raising hackles by serving them in a slightly more civilized manner.

Replace the usual hen eggs with quail eggs, and a robust picnic favourite is given a delicate, elegant makeover.

scotch quail eggs

24 quail eggs
60 g (1/2 cup) plain (all-purpose) flour
600 g (1 lb 5 oz) minced (ground) chicken
2 tbs chopped chives
2 tsp grated fresh ginger
2 tsp Dijon mustard
2 eggs, lightly beaten
100 g (1 cup) dry breadcrumbs
oil, for deep-frying

You can hard-boil quail eggs in the same way you would hen eggs, but they look best if the yolk is centred, and there's a little trick to this. Put the eggs in a saucepan and cover with water. Warm the water over medium heat and keep stirring the eggs gently until the water starts to boil. Then, cook for 5 minutes on the boil. Drain. To cool them, sit them in a bowl of cold water. Next, peel the eggs, and toss them lightly in the flour.

Now move onto the coating: mix the chicken, chives, ginger and mustard in a small bowl. Divide this mixture into 24 even portions, then wrap a portion around each egg — much easier if you have damp hands. Brush each wrapped egg with the beaten egg and then roll in the breadcrumbs, shaking off any excess crumby bits.

Deep-fry the coated eggs until deep golden brown, then drain on crumpled paper towels. Serve hot, either whole or cut in half so that you can admire those centred yolks. Makes 24 whole eggs or 48 halves.

fried calamari with tartare sauce

For the fried calamari:
1 kg (2 lb 4 oz) small, cleaned
squid tubes, thinly sliced
4 tbs cornflour (cornstarch)
4 eggs, lightly beaten
2 garlic cloves, crushed
1 tbs grated lemon zest
200 g (2 cups) dry breadcrumbs
oil, for deep-frying

For the tartare sauce:
250 g (1 cup) mayonnaise
2 small pickled onions, finely chopped
2 tbs chopped chives
1 tbs seeded mustard

To stop your calamari rings behaving like rubber bands, make sure you peel the membrane off the inside of the squid rings. The squid needs to be coated in batter before being cooked, so put the cornflour in one bowl, combine the egg, garlic and lemon zest in another one, and the breadcrumbs in a third. Now dip the squid into each bowl in the same order as above, ending up with well-coated squid.

Deep-fry the squid in batches until just heated through and lightly browned — this will only take a minute or so. Lift the squid out of the oil with a slotted spoon, then drain on crumpled paper towels while you cook the rest of the squid.

There's not much to tartare sauce — simply combine the mayonnaise, pickled onions, chives and mustard. Serve with the calamari. Serves 8.

Don't overcook your squid or it will become chewy, and there's nothing worse than trying to digest little rings of rubber. Just show it to the oil for no more than a minute, and it'll be as good as you get from your local fish-and-chip shop.

Serve your pâté with neat Melba toasts made by toasting a slice of bread, splitting it down the centre and toasting it again.

chicken liver pâté

500 g (1 lb 2 oz) chicken livers, trimmed
4 tbs brandy
90 g (3¼ oz) unsalted butter
1 onion, finely chopped
1 garlic clove, crushed
1 tsp chopped thyme
3 tbs thick (double/heavy) cream

Rinse the livers under cold running water, then dry them with paper towels. Now, cut them in half. Put the liver halves in a small bowl with the brandy, cover with plastic wrap and leave for a couple of hours. Drain the livers, but don't throw out the brandy.

Melt some of the butter, about half, in a frying pan, then throw in the onion and garlic and cook over low heat until the onion is soft and transparent. Add the livers and thyme and stir over medium heat until the livers change colour. Pour in the reserved brandy and let it simmer away for a couple of minutes. Now let it cool for a few minutes.

Put the livers and all those delicious cooking juices in a food processor and whiz smooth. Add the rest of the butter and process again. Pour in the cream and mix it in briefly.

The last step is to season the pâté and scoop it into your most retro earthenware dish or terrine, smoothing the surface. If you want your pâté to look its best, a layer of melted butter will stop the surface going grey. Cover with plastic wrap and refrigerate until firm. Serve with Melba toasts.
Serves 6.

barbecued honey chicken wings

12 chicken wings
4 tbs soy sauce
3 tbs sherry
3 tbs oil
1 garlic clove, crushed
3 tbs honey

Rinse the chicken wings, then give them a thorough pat with paper towels to dry them. Tuck the wing tips to the underside.

Put the chicken wings in a shallow non-metallic dish. Whisk together the soy sauce, sherry, oil and garlic, then pour all over the chicken wings, lightly tossing for good measure. Cover with plastic wrap, then leave in the fridge for 2 hours to give the chicken a chance to take up some of the marinade — it will help if you turn the wings occasionally.

The honey needs to be heated enough for it to become brushing consistency — either use the microwave or warm it gently in a small saucepan.

Lightly grease a barbecue or chargrill pan (griddle) and heat it up. Lift the chicken out of the marinade and add it to the hot pan. Cook the chicken wings until tender and cooked through, turning occasionally — this should take about 12 minutes. Now brush the wings with the warmed honey and cook for 2 minutes more. Serve with a pile of serviettes (napkins) for sticky fingers.
Serves 4.

These make great party food, but to avoid bones in your pot plants, supply a few empty bowls for leftovers.

Dine at a Chinese restaurant and someone's bound to order these as a starter. This recipe makes such good-quality springers that you shouldn't be surprised if you're taking orders for Crispy-skin chicken and Sweet and sour pork to follow.

spring rolls

For the filling:
100 ml (3$^1/_2$ fl oz) soy sauce
3$^1/_2$ tbs Chinese rice wine
2 tsp sesame oil
1$^1/_2$ tsp cornflour (cornstarch)
450 g (1 lb) centre-cut pork loin, trimmed
and cut into very thin strips
6 dried Chinese mushrooms
4 tbs oil
1 tbs finely chopped fresh ginger
3 garlic cloves, finely chopped
125 g (4$^1/_2$ oz) Chinese cabbage,
finely shredded
150 g (5$^1/_2$ oz) carrot, finely shredded
30 g (1 oz) Chinese garlic chives, cut into
2 cm ($^3/_4$ inch) lengths
175 g (6 oz) bean sprouts

1 egg yolk
2 tbs plain (all-purpose) flour
20 square spring roll wrappers
oil, for deep-frying
plum sauce

To make the filling, combine half the soy sauce, rice wine and sesame oil and 1 teaspoon of the cornflour. Mix in the pork and marinate for 20 minutes. At the same time, soak the mushrooms in boiling water for 20 minutes, then drain and squeeze. Discard the stems and shred the caps. Combine the remaining soy sauce, sesame oil and cornflour with pepper.

Stir-fry the pork mixture in half the oil in a wok until cooked, then drain. Clean and reheat the wok. Add the rest of the oil and stir-fry the mushrooms, ginger and garlic briefly. Toss in the cabbage and carrot, then pour in the rest of the rice wine and cook for a minute. Add the garlic chives and sprouts and cook until the sprouts go limp. Add the pork and soy sauce mixtures and cook until thickened. Drain in a colander for 5 minutes.

Combine the egg yolk, flour and 3 tablespoons water. Put 2 tablespoons of filling near the corner of a wrapper. Spread some of the yolk mixture on the opposite corner. Fold over one corner and start rolling. Fold in the side corners and roll up. Do the same with the rest, then deep-fry in batches, turning constantly, for 5 minutes. Drain, then serve with plum sauce. Makes 20.

for starters

Sundae glasses are the ultimate prawn cocktail accessory — if you don't have any buried at the back of your hostess trolley then trot down to your local flea-market for a rummage.

prawn cocktail

250 g (1 cup) mayonnaise
2 tbs tomato sauce
2 tbs thick (double/heavy) cream
1 tsp lemon juice
1 tsp Worcestershire sauce
dash of Tabasco sauce
24 cooked medium prawns (shrimp),
peeled and deveined
iceberg lettuce
lemon wedges
buttered brown bread

Mix the mayonnaise, tomato sauce, cream, lemon juice, Worcestershire sauce and Tabasco together to make a fabulously pink sauce. Keep eight of the most handsome prawns aside for a garnish and pull the tails off the others. Toss the prawns with the sauce.

Arrange the lettuce artistically in individual serving dishes and spoon some of the prawns into each one. Decorate with the reserved prawns — hang a couple over the edge of each dish for a truly retro look. Serve with lemon wedges and bread.
Serves 4.

43

cream of asparagus soup

750 g (1 lb 10 oz) asparagus spears
60 g (2¼ oz) butter
1 small onion, chopped
1 celery stalk, chopped
30 g (¼ cup) plain (all-purpose) flour
750 ml (3 cups) chicken stock
170 ml (²/3 cup) whipping cream
chervil

Cut the tips off the asparagus spears, then finely chop the spears. Drop the tips into a saucepan of boiling salted water for 1 minute, then drain.

Heat the butter in a large saucepan. When it's sizzling, cook the onion, celery and chopped asparagus spears for 5 minutes until the onion is soft — stir often while it's cooking. Now stir in the flour. Remove the pan from the heat, then pour in the stock and give everything a good stir. Return the pan to the hob, pop the lid on and simmer for 20–25 minutes, just until the vegetables are tender. Now drop in the asparagus tips and simmer for another 5 minutes. Cool slightly.

Transfer the mixture to a food processor or blender and blitz in small batches until you have a smooth purée. Return the newly smooth soup to the pan, pour in the cream and swirl until the soup is piping hot. Serve with a jaunty sprig of chervil, if desired. Serves 4–6.

Choose thin, tender asparagus spears rather than those with thick, woody stems for the very best flavour in this soup.

Originally prepared roadside and popular among travelling Spanish mule drivers, this cold tomato soup is at its most authentic served in a large clay bowl with garlic croutons and raw vegetables ... mules to set the scene are optional.

gazpacho

For the soup:

1 kg (2 lb 4 oz) vine-ripened tomatoes
2 slices of day-old white Italian bread,
crust removed, broken into pieces
1 red capsicum (pepper), seeded and
roughly chopped
2 garlic cloves, chopped
1 small green chilli, chopped (optional)
1 tsp sugar
2 tbs red wine vinegar
2 tbs extra virgin olive oil
8 ice cubes

For the garnish:

half a Lebanese (short) cucumber,
seeded and finely diced
half a red capsicum (pepper),
seeded and finely diced
half a green capsicum (pepper),
seeded and finely diced
half a red onion, finely diced
half a ripe tomato, diced

Start by preparing the tomatoes: score a cross in the base of each one, then leave them in a bowl of boiling water for 30 seconds. Now plunge them into cold water before slipping the skins off. Halve them, scoop out the seeds and chop the flesh.

Soak the bread in cold water for 5 minutes, then squeeze really well with your hands. Put the bread in a food processor with the tomato, capsicum, garlic, chilli, sugar and vinegar and blitz until you have a vivid red, smooth purée. With the motor running, slowly pour in the oil to make a smooth, creamy mixture. Season to taste.

Gazpacho is served cold so it will need at least a couple of hours in the fridge to reach a nicely chilled state. Once the soup is chilled, taste a little and add a splash of extra vinegar, if you think it needs it.

To make the garnish, mix the ingredients in a bowl. Put 2 ice cubes in each bowl of soup and serve the garnish separately.
Serves 4.

carpaccio

700 g (1 lb 9 oz) best-quality beef fillet
1 egg yolk
3 tsp Dijon mustard
3 tbs lemon juice
2 drops of Tabasco sauce
4 tbs olive oil
1 tbs cream
2–3 tbs capers, rinsed and squeezed dry

Carpaccio is very thin slices of raw meat — the thinner and more paper-like the slices the better. The secret is to freeze the beef for about half an hour then cut it with a really sharp, large knife. Cover six serving plates with the beef in an even layer.

Now for the sauce. Blend together the egg yolk, mustard, lemon juice and Tabasco in a bowl or food processor. Add the olive oil in a thin stream, whisking or processing continuously until the mayonnaise thickens. Whisk in the cream. Season to taste with salt and pepper. Drizzle over the beef slices and sprinkle with capers.
Serves 6.

Named after the Renaissance painter who loved to use really vivid reds in his paintings. Use the best quality beef and you'll achieve the same effect.

One of those comfort foods that's best eaten in front of a roaring fire on a cold night with a generous hunk of fresh, crusty bread.

roast pumpkin soup

1.25 kg (2 lb 12 oz) pumpkin, peeled
and cut into chunks
2 tbs olive oil
1 large onion, chopped
2 tsp ground cumin
1 large carrot, chopped
1 celery stalk, chopped
1 litre (4 cups) chicken or vegetable stock
sour cream
finely chopped parsley
freshly grated nutmeg

Toss the pumpkin on a greased baking tray with half the olive oil or, if you prefer, use a pastry brush to brush the chunks. Pop the tray in a 180°C (350°F/Gas 4) oven for 25 minutes until the pumpkin starts to go soft and caramel brown around the edges.

Heat the rest of the oil in a large saucepan, then throw in the onion and cumin. Cook this for a couple of minutes, then add the carrot and celery and cook for another 3 minutes, stirring often. Add the roasted pumpkin and stock. Give a brisk stir, bring to the boil, then reduce the heat and simmer for 20 minutes.

Take the pan off the heat and let it cool a little so that the mixture doesn't splatter everywhere when you're blending. Scoop the mixture into a blender or food processor and blitz until you have a smooth soup. Return the soup to the pan and gently reheat without boiling. Season to taste with salt and freshly ground black pepper. Top with a dollop of sour cream, and sprinkle with chopped parsley and nutmeg before serving. Serves 6.

french onion soup

50 g (1³/4 oz) butter
750 g (1 lb 10 oz) onions, finely sliced
2 garlic cloves, finely chopped
4 tbs plain (all-purpose) flour
2 litres (8 cups) beef or chicken stock
250 ml (1 cup) white wine
1 bay leaf
2 thyme sprigs
12 slices stale baguette
100 g (3½ oz) Gruyère, finely grated

The secret to a really good French onion soup is to take your time when cooking the onion so that the flavour is rich and mellow. Take a heavy-based saucepan and melt the butter in it. Toss in the onion then cook over low heat, stirring occasionally, for 25 minutes, or until the onion is deep golden brown and beginning to caramelize; a glass of wine in hand will make time pass pleasantly.

Now add the garlic and flour and stir continuously for 2 minutes. Gradually blend in the stock and the wine, stirring all the time, and bring to the boil. Add the bay leaf and thyme and season. Cover the pan and simmer for 25 minutes. Remove the bay leaf and thyme and check the seasoning. Preheat the grill.

Toast the baguette slices, then divide among six warmed soup bowls and ladle the soup over the top. Sprinkle with the grated cheese and grill until the cheese melts and turns light golden brown. Serve immediately.
Serves 6.

While it may be considered bad form to dunk your bread in your soup, there's no denying that it tastes delicious. A slice of toast in the bottom of each bowl of French onion soup neatly gets around the etiquette problem.

It's easy to imagine Professor Henry Higgins teaching Eliza Doolittle the niceties of pronouncing, then eating, this cold leek and potato soup.

vichyssoise

4 leeks, trimmed and cut into 4 lengthways
30 g (1 oz) butter
3 floury potatoes, peeled and chopped
750 ml (3 cups) chicken or vegetable stock
250 ml (1 cup) milk
1/4 tsp freshly grated nutmeg
cream
chopped spring onions (scallions)

To make sure you get rid of any dirt lurking in the leeks, wash them thoroughly in cold water, then cut into small chunks. Melt the butter in a large heavy-based saucepan, add the leek and cook gently for 3–4 minutes until soft. Next, add the potato and stock. Bring the mixture slowly to the boil, then reduce the heat and simmer for about 20 minutes until the vegetables are tender.

Blenders often don't cope well with very hot mixtures, so let the mixture cool for a couple of minutes, then purée until smooth — depending on the size of your blender, you might need to do this in a couple of batches. Stir in the milk, nutmeg and some salt and freshly ground black pepper. Chill really well, then serve garnished with a swirl of cream and a scattering of spring onion.
Serves 4.

garlic prawns

6 garlic cloves, crushed
1–2 small red chillies, very finely chopped
250 ml (1 cup) olive oil
60 g (2¼ oz) butter
24 large prawns (shrimp), peeled and
deveined, with the tails intact
2 tbs chopped parsley

Sprinkle the garlic and chilli into four cast-iron or gratin dishes. Divide the oil and butter among the dishes.

Put the dishes on a baking tray in a 220°C (425°F/Gas 7) oven and heat until the butter has melted — 5 minutes should do.

Divide the prawns among the dishes (use a light touch so the oil doesn't splash) and bake in the oven until the prawns are coral coloured and tender — this will take less than 10 minutes. Sprinkle with parsley and serve immediately with crusty bread to soak up the gorgeously naughty buttery oil.
Serves 4.

These prawns taste so good that you really have to be sure to devour every last morsel. Put some finger bowls on the table with a couple of flowers floating in them for a delicate touch, then watch everyone dig in with unrestrained gusto.

One of those dishes where you don't know whether to try to fit a little of everything on your fork, or go for each piece individually. Either way, it's sublime.

prawn mango salad

For the dressing:
2 tbs sour cream
175 g (6 oz) can mango purée
3 tbs lime juice
1 tbs sweet chilli sauce

For the salad:
6 bacon rashers, chopped
2 kg (4$^{1}/_{2}$ lb) cooked king prawns (shrimp),
peeled and deveined, with the tails intact
3 large mangoes, peeled and
cut into thin wedges
2 large avocados, sliced

The dressing is a cinch — combine all the ingredients in a small bowl and whisk until smooth.

Fry the bacon until crispy, then drain on paper towels.

Arrange the prawns, mango and avocado on a large platter, then sprinkle with the bacon bits. Drizzle with the dressing, then serve. Serves 6.

the main event

When it's cold outside, a steaming bowl of apricot chicken will warm the soul.

apricot chicken

1 tbs oil

1.5 kg (3 lb 5 oz) skinless chicken thigh fillets, trimmed and cut into 2.5 cm (1 inch) pieces

120 g ($2/3$ cup) dried apricots, cut into strips

375 ml ($1^1/2$ cups) apricot nectar

170 ml ($2/3$ cup) chicken stock

40 g (1 sachet) dried French onion soup mix

1 tbs finely chopped parsley

First of all, heat the oil in a large frying pan or flameproof casserole dish. When the oil gets really hot, cook the chicken — in two batches — over medium heat until each piece is a lovely golden brown colour all over. Drain off any fat left in the pan, then return all the chicken pieces to the pan.

Add the apricot strips, apricot nectar, stock and soup mix to the pan and stir around until everything is mixed together. Bring to the boil, then reduce the heat, cover with a lid and simmer gently for 10 minutes. Take off the lid and cook for another 5–10 minutes, stirring occasionally until the chicken is tender and the sauce is slightly thickened.

Remove the pan from the heat before stirring in the parsley. This is good served piping hot with steamed green vegetables and chunks of crusty bread.
Serves 6.

spaghetti bolognese

2 tbs olive oil
2 garlic cloves, crushed
1 large onion, chopped
1 carrot, finely chopped
1 celery stalk, finely chopped
500 g (1 lb 2 oz) lean minced (ground) beef
500 ml (2 cups) beef stock
375 ml (1½ cups) red wine
2 x 425 g (15 oz) cans chopped tomatoes
1 tsp sugar
3 tbs parsley, finely chopped
500 g (1 lb 2 oz) spaghetti
grated Parmesan cheese

Heat some olive oil in a large, deep frying pan, then add the garlic, onion, carrot and celery and stir over low heat for 5 minutes until the vegetables are just starting to become tender.

Increase the heat of the hob before adding the beef. You'll need to stir the meat to break up any lumps — a wooden spoon is good for this. Once the meat is nicely browned, add the stock, wine, tomatoes, sugar and parsley. Bring to the boil, then reduce the heat and simmer for 1½ hours or thereabouts, stirring occasionally. Season with salt and freshly ground black pepper.

Shortly before serving, cook the spaghetti in a large saucepan of rapidly boiling, salted water until *al dente*. Drain and serve with the meat sauce and the Parmesan cheese. Serves 4–6.

We now all know that the Italians always serve their bolognese with tagliatelle, but who said tradition is everything?

Give the evening a Japanese theme by seating everyone on cushions on the floor and getting them to practise their skill with chopsticks. Don't forget to pass around the sake.

teppanyaki

350 g (12 oz) scotch fillet
assorted vegetables, such as green beans,
slender eggplant (aubergine), shiitake
mushrooms, red or green capsicum
(pepper), spring onions (scallions)
12 prawns (shrimp), peeled and deveined,
with tails intact
3 tbs oil
soy sauce

First, you need to slice the meat very thinly. The secret to this is to partially freeze the meat (about 30 minutes should be enough), then slice it with a very sharp knife. Place the meat slices in a single layer on a large serving platter and season well with salt and pepper.

Cut the vegetables into long, thin strips, then arrange them in separate bundles on a plate. Arrange the prawns on a third plate.

The idea with teppanyaki is to cook the meal at the table on a very hot electric grill (griddle) or frying pan. Lightly brush the pan with the oil. Quickly fry about a quarter of the meat, searing on both sides, and then push it over to the edge of the pan while you cook about a quarter of the vegetables and the prawns. Serve a small portion of the meat and vegetables to the diners, who dip the food into soy sauce. Repeat the process with the remaining meat and vegetables, cooking in batches as extra helpings are required. Serve with rice.
Serves 4.

steak diane

4 x 200 g (7 oz) fillet steaks
2 garlic cloves, crushed
40 g (1½ oz) butter
4 spring onions (scallions), finely chopped
2 tsp Dijon mustard
2 tbs Worcestershire sauce
1 tbs brandy
4 tbs whipping cream
2 tbs finely chopped parsley
handful of chives

Bash the steaks to about 1.5 cm (5/8 inch) thick. Smear some garlic over the steaks, then sprinkle with pepper. Melt most of the butter in a heavy-based frying pan and when it's hot, cook the steaks over high heat for 2–4 minutes on each side, depending on how you like your steak. When they're cooked to your liking, take them out of the pan, cover with foil and rest somewhere warm.

Heat the rest of the butter in the pan and cook the spring onion for 2 minutes. Add the mustard, Worcestershire sauce and brandy and stir briskly so any crusty bits from the bottom come loose. Swirl in the cream, then simmer for 5 minutes until you have a lusciously rich sauce.

Return the steaks to the pan with the parsley to warm through. Scatter with some chives and serve with sautéed potatoes.
Serves 4.

If you're slimming, leave out the cream and add 1 teaspoon lemon juice and 4 tablespoons chicken stock, instead.

Steak Diane was once the darling of grand hotel dining rooms where it would have been prepared tableside. So ferret out some lapels and a white blazer and spend an evening at the Savoy.

This is a meal best enjoyed with a few good friends and a couple of bottles of red wine. Try to do it on a Friday or Saturday night, as it's the type of dinner party that's still going strong the next morning.

lasagne

For the meat sauce:
1 tbs olive oil
750 g (1 lb 10 oz) minced (ground) beef
1 onion, finely chopped
1 celery stalk, finely chopped
425 g (15 oz) can chopped tomatoes
2 tbs tomato paste (purée)
1 tsp dried mixed herbs
1–2 tsp sugar

For the béchamel sauce:
60 g (2¼ oz) butter
30 g (¼ cup) plain (all-purpose) flour
750 ml (3 cups) milk

375 g (13 oz) packet fresh lasagne
125 g (1 cup) grated vintage Cheddar cheese

Heat half the oil in a large frying pan and brown the beef in batches. Remove all the meat from the pan and set aside on a plate. Heat the rest of the oil, then cook the onion and celery until soft and golden. Return the beef to the pan and stir in the tomato, tomato paste, dried herbs and sugar. Let the mixture come to the boil, then reduce the heat and simmer with a lid on for 20 minutes.

Move onto the béchamel. Melt the butter in a saucepan over low heat. Stir in the flour and cook until it is pale and foaming. Remove from the heat and gradually stir in the milk. Return to the heat and stir constantly until the sauce boils and thickens. Reduce the heat and simmer for another 2 minutes.

To assemble, build layers in a lightly greased 2.5 litre (10 cup) ovenproof dish. Start with one-third of the meat sauce, next add a layer of the lasagne sheets (you might need to trim them), then finish with one-third of the béchamel. Repeat until everything is used up. For the finishing touch, sprinkle with Cheddar, then pop into a 180°C (350°F/Gas 4) oven and bake for 25 minutes until golden.
Serves 6.

beef and kidney bean burrito bake

For the filling:
1 tbs oil

1 green chilli, seeded and finely chopped

1 red onion, chopped

500 g (1 lb 2 oz) lean minced (ground) beef

425 g (15 oz) can kidney beans, drained and rinsed

425 g (15 oz) can chopped tomatoes

450 g (1 lb) can refried beans

1 tsp cumin seeds

1/2 tsp garam masala

4 x 30 cm (12 inch) flour tortillas

4 tbs sour cream

125 g (1 cup) grated Cheddar cheese

To make the filling, start by heating the oil in a large frying pan. Next, add the chilli and onion and stir for 1 minute. Increase the heat, then add the beef and cook for about 5 minutes. While it's cooking, use a wooden spoon or fork to break up any lumps. Stir in the kidney beans, chopped tomatoes, refried beans, cumin seeds and garam masala. Reduce the heat and simmer gently for about half an hour, stirring occasionally.

Divide the filling into four equal portions and spoon one portion down the centre of each tortilla. Then roll the tortilla up to enclose the filling.

Sit the filled tortillas seam-side down in a lightly greased large ovenproof dish, spread evenly with the sour cream and sprinkle with Cheddar cheese. Bake in a 180°C (350°F/Gas 4) oven until the cheese has melted and started to brown and the burritos are slightly crispy — this could take from 20 to 25 minutes. Serve hot with a salad.
Serves 4.

This rich, cheesy dish is the ultimate in comfort food. It's great for entertaining because it's so easy. Just serve with a couple of salads to add some crunch.

If you can't have fish and chips sitting on the beach on a glorious day, then fish pie at home is the next best thing.

fish pie

500 g (2 large) potatoes, peeled and chopped
1 egg
60 g (2¼ oz) butter
440 ml (1¾ cups) milk
60 g (½ cup) grated Cheddar cheese
800 g (1 lb 12 oz) white fish fillets,
cut into large chunks
1 onion, finely chopped
1 garlic clove, crushed
2 tbs plain (all-purpose) flour
2 tbs lemon juice
2 tsp lemon zest

The first step is to cook the potatoes until tender. Now drain them well and mash with the egg, half the butter and 3 tablespoons of the milk. Mix in half the cheese, then set aside somewhere warm.

Put the fish in a shallow frying pan and cover with the rest of the milk. Bring to the boil, then reduce the heat and simmer for about 2 minutes until the flesh flakes when tested with a knife. Lift the fish out of the pan, but don't throw away the milk.

Melt the remaining butter over medium heat in a small saucepan and cook the onion and garlic for 2 minutes. Stir in the flour and cook for a minute until pale and foaming. Remove from the heat and gradually stir in the reserved milk. Return to the heat and stir constantly until the sauce boils and thickens, then reduce the heat and simmer for 2 minutes. Add the lemon juice and zest, then season.

Put the fish into a 1.5 litre (6 cup) ovenproof dish and gently mix in the sauce. Spoon the potato over the fish and top with the rest of the cheese. Bake in a 180°C (350°F/Gas 4) oven for 35 minutes until the top is golden. Serves 4.

pepper steak

4 x 200 g (7 oz) fillet steaks
2 tbs oil
6 tbs black peppercorns, crushed
40 g (1½ oz) butter
3 tbs Cognac or brandy
125 ml (½ cup) thick (double/heavy) cream

Rub the steaks on both sides with the oil and press the crushed peppercorns into the meat so they don't come off while you're frying. Melt the butter in a large frying pan and cook the steaks for 2–4 minutes on each side, depending on how you like your steak.

Now for the fun part: add the Cognac or brandy and flambé by lighting the pan with your gas flame or a match (stand well back when you do this and keep a pan lid handy for emergencies). Lift the steaks out onto a hot plate. Add the wine to the pan and boil, stirring, for 1 minute to deglaze the pan. Add the cream and stir for a couple of minutes. Season with salt and pepper and pour over the steaks.
Serves 4.

Still seen on pub menus everywhere, but you don't necessarily have to go out to eat a hearty steak with a good pepper sauce. Serve with a selection of roasted vegetables.

The famed blue ribbon (*cordon bleu*) was awarded to food prepared to the highest of standards, making this delicious combination of ham and cheese stuffed into chicken a definite winner.

chicken cordon bleu

4 large chicken breast
fillets, trimmed
4 slices of Swiss cheese
4 thin slices of ham
60 g (1/2 cup) plain (all-purpose) flour
1 large egg, beaten
65 g (2/3 cup) seasoned fine
dry breadcrumbs
2 tbs oil

The object of this recipe is to cut a pocket in the chicken and fill it with ham and cheese. To do this, use a sharp knife and cut a deep pocket in each breast half, cutting from the thinnest into the thickest part without cutting all the way through. Open the chicken out flat, then season with some salt and pepper. Put a slice of cheese and ham on one side of each breast (you might need to cut them to fit if they're too big). Fold the remaining half of breast over to enclose the filling, pressing down to enclose the ham and cheese.

Now coat the chicken 'sandwiches', first in flour, then in egg and, finally, in breadcrumbs. Put on a foil-lined baking tray in the fridge for about half an hour.

In a large frying pan, heat the oil. Cook the chicken over medium heat for 4–5 minutes on each side until the chicken is golden and cooked through. You might find that you need to add a bit more oil to the pan, so keep it on hand. Serve immediately.
Serves 4.

fajitas

185 ml (3/4 cup) olive oil
2 tbs lime juice
4 garlic cloves, chopped
3 red chillies, chopped
2 tbs tequila (optional)
1 kg (2 lb 4 oz) rump steak,
thinly sliced into strips
1 red and yellow capsicum (pepper),
thinly sliced
1 red onion, thinly sliced
8 flour tortillas
guacamole
shredded lettuce
diced tomato
sour cream

First make a marinade out of the oil, lime juice, garlic, chilli, tequila and some pepper. Add the meat, cover and marinate it for several hours or overnight, if you have time.

Drain the meat and toss it with the capsicum and onion. Around the time that you want to eat, wrap the tortillas in foil and warm them in a 150°C (300°F/Gas 2) oven for about 5 minutes. Cook the meat and vegetables in batches in a sizzling hot heavy-based frying pan until cooked, then scoop onto a serving plate and sit in the middle of the table with the tortillas, guacamole, shredded lettuce, diced tomato and sour cream. Let everyone assemble their own fajita.
Serves 4.

Serve the fajitas with homemade guacamole if you've got a spare few minutes, by mashing together avocado, lime juice, chilli, salt and spring onion (scallion). Easy to make, and so much nicer than a shop-bought dip.

Dig out your fondue set, throw away any calorific concerns and settle down to a cheesefest — served, of course, with lashings of red wine.

cheese fondue

half a garlic clove
1 bottle dry white wine
520 g (4 cups) grated Gruyère cheese
520 g (4 cups) grated Emmental cheese
2 tbs cornflour (cornstarch)
shot of kirsch
pinch of freshly grated nutmeg
cubes of bread

Rub the inside of a fondue pot with the garlic. Pour in the wine and bring it to the boil. Stir in the cheese and cornflour and melt it slowly, stirring constantly. Fire up the fondue burner and lift on the pot, then stir in the kirsch and nutmeg.

The rules of fondue are simple. The bread cube goes on the end of the fork which then gets dunked in the cheese — dropping your bread into the cheese is a no no which usually merits a forfeit.
Serves 6.

steak with green peppercorn sauce

4 x 200 g (7 oz) fillet steaks
30 g (1 oz) butter
2 tsp oil
250 ml (1 cup) beef stock
185 ml (3/4 cup) whipping cream
2 tsp cornflour (cornstarch)
2 tbs green peppercorns in brine, rinsed and drained
2 tbs brandy

First of all, bash the steaks with a meat mallet to 1.5 cm (5/8 inch) thick — a very therapeutic job if you're stressed. Next, nick the edges of the steaks to prevent them from curling when they are cooking.

Heat the butter and oil in a heavy-based frying pan over high heat, then fry the steaks for 2–4 minutes on each side, depending on how you like your steak. Transfer to a serving plate and cover with foil.

Now add the stock to the pan juices and stir over low heat until boiling. Combine the cream and cornflour, then pour the mixture into the pan and stir constantly until the sauce becomes smooth and thick — a few minutes will do the trick. Add the peppercorns and brandy and boil for 1 more minute before taking the pan off the heat. Spoon the sauce over the steaks.
Serves 4.

'Woe to the cook whose sauce has no sting', said fourteenth century poet Geoffrey Chaucer, who no doubt would have enjoyed the bite in a peppercorn sauce. Seven centuries later, we can still appreciate his words.

One of those dishes where less is definitely more, a Wiener schnitzel needs only a squeeze of lemon juice to perfect it.

wiener schnitzel

4 thin veal steaks, trimmed
4 tbs plain (all-purpose) flour
1 egg, lightly beaten
100 g (1 cup) dry breadcrumbs
3 tbs oil
30 g (1 oz) butter
1 lemon, sliced

First flatten the steaks by smacking them with a meat mallet or rolling pin — ideally, they should be 5 mm (1/4 inch) thick. Next nick the edges to prevent them from curling. Now pat the meat dry with paper towels.

The idea is to coat the steaks in a crumb coating before you cook them. Start off by coating them lightly in seasoned flour, then shake off any excess. Next, dip the steak into egg and, finally, finish with a coating of breadcrumbs, which should stick on. Put the crumbed steaks on a foil-lined tray, cover and refrigerate for at least 30 minutes.

Heat the oil and butter in a large frying pan over medium heat, then cook the veal for 3 minutes on each side until golden. Serve with lemon. Some steamed baby potatoes would also be great with this.
Serves 4.

steak tartare

250 g (9 oz) best-quality fillet steak, trimmed
2 egg yolks
2 tbs capers, rinsed and squeezed dry
2 tbs finely chopped onion
4 anchovy fillets, drained and mashed
rye bread

Chop or mince the meat very finely just before you're ready to eat. Shape the meat into two mounds and place in the centre of two serving dishes. Make a well in the centre of each mound and gently place a whole egg yolk in each well.

Serve capers, onion, anchovies and salt and pepper separately to accompany the steak so that each person can combine the flavours to suit themselves. Serve with rye bread.
Serves 2.

Why dress up a good dish if it doesn't need it? Give in to your primal instincts and enjoy your dinner in the raw.

The trout is best brought as fresh as possible from swimming in the river to swimming in lemon butter on your plate.

trout with almonds

2 rainbow trout, washed and patted dry
plain (all-purpose) flour
60 g (2¼ oz) butter
3 tbs flaked almonds
2 tbs lemon juice
1 tbs finely chopped parsley

If you've got an obliging fishmonger, ask him to bone the trout for you. Otherwise, it's quite simple to do yourself. Start by opening the trout out skin-side up. Gently run a rolling pin along the backbone starting at the tail. Now turn the trout over and cut through the backbone at each end of the fish with a pair of kitchen scissors. Lever the backbone out, and look carefully for any remaining bones — tweezers are helpful for getting rid of these. Lastly, trim the fins with scissors.

Lightly toss the fish in flour and shake off any excess. In a large frying pan, heat half of the butter. Cook the fish for 4 minutes on each side until golden brown. Remove the fish from the pan and place on heated serving plates. Cover them with foil while you make the sauce.

Heat the rest of the butter in the pan, then add the flaked almonds and stir until the almonds are light golden brown — watch them carefully so they don't burn. Add the lemon juice, parsley, some salt and pepper and stir until the sauce is heated through. Pour over the trout and serve immediately. Serves 2.

veal cordon bleu

8 thin veal steaks, trimmed
4 thin slices of ham
4 slices of Gruyère or Emmental cheese
plain (all-purpose) flour
2 eggs, lightly beaten
200 g (2 cups) dry breadcrumbs
30 g (1 oz) butter
3 tbs olive oil

The idea of this recipe is to make a kind of sandwich, with the veal steaks taking the place of bread. To begin, flatten the steaks to 5 mm (¼ inch) thick. Lay a slice of ham or prosciutto and a slice of cheese on four of the steaks. Complete the sandwich by topping with the remaining steaks. To keep the sandwiches together, they need to be coated, first in lightly seasoned flour, then in egg and, lastly, in breadcrumbs. Cover and refrigerate for at least 30 minutes.

Heat the butter and oil in a large heavy-based frying pan and, when hot, cook the veal over medium heat for about 3 minutes. Carefully turn and cook for another 3 minutes until golden. Drain on paper towels. Serve with steamed vegetables.
Serves 4.

The delicate flavour of veal combines beautifully with ham and cheese to make this a prize-winning favourite.

So many delicious tastes packed neatly into a pocket of steak. The memory of this meal is one you'll always carry with you.

carpetbag steak

4 rib eye steaks, each 4 cm (1¹/₂ inches)
thick, trimmed
8 oysters, shelled
1 tsp chopped parsley
2 tsp lemon juice
2 tbs oil
250 ml (1 cup) beef stock
2 tsp Worcestershire sauce
60 g (2¹/₄ oz) butter, diced

The aim of this recipe is to make a pocket in the steaks and fill them with goodies. Take a sharp knife and cut a deep incision into the side of each steak. Combine the oysters, parsley, lemon juice and a little pepper in a bowl, then spoon some of this mixture into the pocket in each steak. Use a few toothpicks to close up the pocket so that the filling doesn't spill out when you're cooking.

Heat the oil in a frying pan and cook the steaks over high heat for 3–6 minutes on each side, depending on how you like your steak. Drain on paper towels. Cover and keep warm.

Bring the stock and Worcestershire sauce to the boil in the pan. Reduce the heat, stir in the butter until it melts, then pour over the steaks. Serve with steamed potatoes. Serves 4.

tournedos rossini

4 fillet steaks, each 3 cm (1¹/4 inches)
thick, patted dry
90 g (3¹/4 oz) butter
1 garlic clove, crushed
4 slices of bread
1 tbs oil
4 slices of pâté 2 cm (³/4 inch) thick
400 g (14 oz) can artichoke hearts,
drained and cut in half
170 ml (²/3 cup) beef stock
1 tsp cornflour (cornstarch)
1 tbs dry Madeira or sherry
2 tbs cream
watercress

Lightly sprinkle the steaks with pepper. Make a fragrant garlicky butter by melting a third of the butter in a small pan with the garlic.

Cut the bread into rounds the same size as the steaks. Lightly brush both sides of the bread with the garlic butter. Toast the bread on a baking tray in a 180°C (350°F/Gas 4) oven for 20 minutes until golden.

Heat the oil and half the remaining butter in a frying pan over high heat, then cook the steaks for 3–7 minutes on each side, depending how you like your steak. Put a piece of pâté on each steak, then cover with foil and rest.

Melt the last of the butter in a clean frying pan and gently toss in the artichoke hearts so they don't break up. Cover and keep warm.

Splash the stock into the steak pan juices and boil rapidly until it has reduced by half. Make a paste out of the cornflour and Madeira and stir it into the pan for a minute or so until the sauce thickens slightly. Stir in the cream and pour the sauce over the steaks. Serve with artichoke hearts and garnish with watercress. Serves 4.

Named after the Italian composer Gioacchino Rossini, the original dish was served with foie gras and truffles. This variation is just as good, but slightly less intimidating.

The ultimate dinner party dish of the 70s and 80s, shamed out of existence in the health-conscious 90s — but in the new millennium chicken Kiev is back!

chicken kiev

125 g (4½ oz) unsalted butter, softened
1 garlic clove, crushed
2 tbs chopped parsley
2 tsp grated lemon zest
2 tsp lemon juice
6 small chicken breast fillets,
tenderloins removed
60 g (½ cup) plain (all-purpose) flour
2 eggs, beaten
200 g (2 cups) dry breadcrumbs
oil, for deep-frying
lemon wedges

The object of this recipe is to stuff chicken breasts with butter and then cook them without the butter escaping — this means the butter must be rock hard to stop it melting.

Mix together the butter, garlic, parsley, lemon zest and juice. Shape it into a rectangle and wrap it in foil. Now chill it until it is rock hard. Flatten the chicken breasts by smacking them (not too hard) with a rolling pin and then cut a pocket in the side of each one.

Cut the chilled butter into six fingers. Put one finger into each chicken pocket and fasten it shut with a toothpick. Toss the Kievs in flour, then egg and, finally, the breadcrumbs which should stick to the egg in a thick layer. They now go back in the fridge for at least 1 hour to chill.

Deep-fry the Kievs for 5 minutes — they should be golden all over. (Don't forget to pull out the toothpicks.). Serve with lemon wedges. Serves 6.

Make life easier for yourself by making them ahead of time and doing the frying at the last minute.

chateaubriand

500 g (1 lb 2 oz) piece of rib eye
steak, trimmed
90 g (3¼ oz) butter
250 ml (1 cup) white wine
6 finely chopped spring onions (scallions)
1 tsp each of chopped tarragon and parsley

Pat the steak dry with paper towels. It will need a helping hand to keep its gorgeous figure, so tie it at intervals with a corset of kitchen string. Roll it in some pepper.

Heat two-thirds of the butter in a heavy-based frying pan. Add the steak and brown all over. Reduce the heat to medium and cook for a further 20–25 minutes, turning frequently. By this time, the meat should be well browned on the outside and rare in the centre. Remove the meat from the pan, cover and keep warm while you move onto preparing the sauce.

Deglaze the pan with wine and let it bubble away until only about 4 tablespoons are left. Heat half the remaining butter in a small frying pan, add the spring onion and let it cook until it is soft — this should only take a couple of minutes. Add to the wine sauce and cook for only a few more minutes. Remove from the heat, then stir in the rest of the butter and the herbs.

To serve, cut the fillet into thick slices. Serve with the sauce, potatoes, asparagus spears and a watercress garnish.
Serves 4.

A chateaubriand is a thick steak cut from a fillet of beef, usually cooked for two people. It's served with a sauce very similar to béarnaise, but without the egg yolks — still tasty, but not quite as rich.

You can save time preparing the chilli by using canned tomatoes if you wish, or preparing it in advance then reheating on the day. If you want to take the healthy option, serve it with a bowl of steamed rice.

chilli con carne

175 g (6 oz) dried kidney beans
650 g (1 lb 7 oz) tomatoes
1 1/2 tbs oil
900 g (2 lb) trimmed chuck steak,
cut into chunks
3 onions, thinly sliced
2 garlic cloves, chopped
2 tsp ground cumin
1 tbs paprika
1/2 tsp ground allspice
1–2 tsp chilli powder
1 tbs soft brown sugar
1 tbs red wine vinegar

Soak the beans in plenty of water overnight. Drain well. Score a cross in the base of each tomato. Put the tomatoes in a bowl of boiling water for 30 seconds, then plunge into a bowl of cold water. Take them out of the water and slip off the skins. Halve the tomatoes and scoop out the seeds. Finely chop the flesh.

Heat most of the oil in a large heavy-based pan and then cook half the meat until well browned, 2 minutes or so. Scoop it onto a plate, then repeat with the rest of the meat.

Cook the onion in the rest of the oil over medium heat until translucent. Add the garlic and spices and stir for a minute or so until aromatic. Pour in 500 ml (2 cups) water and stir well before returning the meat to the pan along with the beans and tomatoes. Bring to the boil, then reduce the heat and simmer, partially covered, stirring occasionally, until the meat is tender and the mixture is thick and dryish — this will take about 2 hours. If the mixture starts to catch on the bottom of the pan, add a little water. Stir in the sugar and vinegar, and season with salt. Delicious with flour tortillas and grated cheese.
Serves 6.

peppered beef fillet with béarnaise sauce

For the peppered beef fillet:
1 kg (2 lb 4 oz) beef eye fillet, trimmed
1 tbs oil
2 garlic cloves, crushed
1 tbs cracked black peppercorns
2 tsp crushed coriander seeds

For the béarnaise sauce:
3 spring onions (scallions), chopped
125 ml (1/2 cup) dry white wine
2 tbs tarragon vinegar
1 tbs chopped tarragon
125 g (4 1/2 oz) butter
4 egg yolks
1 tbs lemon juice

You'll need to tie the beef at intervals with kitchen string to keep it in shape. Combine the oil and garlic, then brush the garlicky oil over the beef before rolling it in the combined peppercorns and coriander seeds.

Sit the meat on a rack in a roasting tin. Bake for 10 minutes in a 210°C (415°F/Gas 6–7) oven, then reduce the temperature to 180°C (350°F/Gas 4) and cook for another 15–30 minutes, depending how you like your meat cooked. Once it is cooked, cover with foil and rest for 10–15 minutes.

To make the béarnaise sauce, put the spring onion, wine, vinegar and tarragon in a small saucepan. Boil rapidly until only 2 tablespoons of the liquid remains, then strain it into a bowl. Melt the butter in a small saucepan. Blitz the wine mixture and egg yolks in a food processor for 30 seconds. With the motor running, add the hot butter in a thin stream and keep whizzing until the sauce is thick. Lastly, stir in the lemon juice and a pinch of salt and white pepper. Serve the beef with the béarnaise sauce, and some roasted vegetables.
Serves 6.

If it didn't mean forsaking the unsurpassed pleasure of sinking your teeth into a really good piece of beef, being a vegetarian would be easy.

Best enjoyed at a Southern-style picnic buffet with long trestle tables groaning with food. It's probably a good idea to loosen the stays on your corset, though.

country-fried chicken

12 chicken drumsticks
4 tbs crushed cornflakes
185 g (1½ cups) plain (all-purpose) flour
2 tbs instant chicken stock powder
1 tsp celery salt
1 tsp onion salt
½ tsp garlic powder
½ tsp ground white pepper
oil

There are two stages to cooking this chicken. The first is to cook the chicken flesh, the next to brown the skin. To begin, bring a large saucepan of water to the boil, then lower the chicken into the pan. Bring the water back to the boil, then reduce the heat to a simmer and leave gently simmering for 15 minutes until the chicken is cooked through. Lift the drumsticks out of the water with tongs.

Make a mixture of the cornflake crumbs, flour, stock powder, celery salt, onion salt, garlic powder and white pepper — this will be the crumb coating for the chicken. Put the drumsticks in a large bowl and cover with water. Dip the wet drumsticks into the crumb mixture and shake off the excess.

In a large saucepan heat 4 cm (1½ inches) oil. Gently lower the chicken drumsticks into the oil, a few at a time. Cook for about 8 minutes, or until they turn a rich golden brown and have a crunchy coating. Carefully remove the chicken from the oil with tongs or a slotted spoon. Drain on paper towels and keep warm. Repeat with the remaining chicken pieces. Serve hot.
Serves 6.

meat loaf

125 g (4¹/2 oz) bacon, trimmed and chopped
500 g (1 lb 2 oz) minced (ground) beef
500 g (1 lb 2 oz) minced (ground) pork
160 g (2 cups) fresh breadcrumbs
1 onion, coarsely grated
2 garlic cloves, crushed
2 tsp thyme leaves
1 egg, lightly beaten
1 tbs red wine vinegar
2 tsp soft brown sugar

Lightly grease a loaf tin, then line with a single sheet of baking paper, leaving the paper to overhang on the long sides of the tin. Heat a non-stick frying pan, add the bacon, and cook until crispy, stirring frequently. Drain on paper towels, then tumble into a large bowl. Add the beef, pork, breadcrumbs, onion, garlic, thyme, egg, vinegar and sugar to the bowl. Season and mix together using your hands, but don't be too energetic or the meat loaf will become too dense when cooked.

Spoon the mixture into the loaf tin and press down gently. Smooth the top and cook it in a 180°C (350°F/Gas 4) oven for 1¹/4 hours, by which stage it should be browned and cooked through. Test if it is cooked by pushing a metal skewer or sharp knife into the centre, leaving it for 3 seconds, and then pulling it out and holding it against your wrist. If it is really hot, it is cooked through; if not, cook a little longer. Leave for 5 minutes and pour the cooking juices into a jug. Lift out the meat loaf using the overhanging baking paper as handles. Cut into slices (a cinch with a serrated knife), then drizzle with the yummy cooking juices.
Serves 6.

Turn any leftover meat loaf into a decadent sandwich with a wedge of cheese, some sliced tomato and shredded lettuce piled mouth-achingly high in a crusty bun.

When you're cooking for friends, you want to impress. So go for the absolute best Parmesan cheese, Parmigiano Reggiano, direct from Italy.

veal parmigiana

4 thin veal steaks, trimmed
plain (all-purpose) flour
1 egg, lightly beaten
1 tbs milk
100 g (1 cup) dry breadcrumbs
3 tbs grated Parmesan cheese
125 ml (1/2 cup) olive oil
100 g (31/2 oz) mozzarella cheese,
grated or thinly sliced
50 g (1/2 cup) grated Parmesan
cheese, extra

For the tomato sauce:
1 tbs oil
1 onion, finely chopped
half a celery stalk, finely chopped
1 carrot, finely chopped
1 small green capsicum (pepper),
finely chopped
1 garlic clove, crushed
425 g (15 oz) can chopped tomatoes
1 tbs tomato paste (purée)
1 tsp dried basil
1 tsp sugar

The steaks need to be flattened, then crumbed. First coat them in flour, then the combined egg and milk and, finally, a mixture of the breadcrumbs and Parmesan with a little salt and pepper for seasoning. Now chill the crumbed veal for at least 30 minutes.

Heat the oil in a large heavy-based pan. Cook the veal in the hot oil over medium heat for 2 minutes on each side until golden brown and cooked through. Drain on paper towels.

To make the tomato sauce, cook the onion, celery, carrot, capsicum and garlic in the hot oil over low heat for 10 minutes, stirring frequently until it's soft. Add the tomatoes, tomato paste, basil and sugar and cook for another half hour or so, stirring often so that it doesn't stick to the pan. Let the sauce cool.

Now for the assembly. Start with a layer of tomato sauce in a large ovenproof dish. Arrange the veal in a single layer on top of the sauce, then spoon the remaining sauce over the veal. Sprinkle mozzarella and Parmesan on top, then pop the whole lot in a 180°C (350°F/Gas 4) oven until the cheese is melted and golden, about 25 minutes. Serves 4.

chicken teriyaki

750 g (1 lb 10 oz) chicken
tenderloins, trimmed
4 tbs soy sauce
3 tbs mirin
3 tbs sherry
3 tbs soft brown sugar
2 tsp grated fresh ginger
1 red capsicum (pepper), cut
into 2 cm (3/4 inch) squares
4 spring onions (scallions), cut into
2.5 cm (1 inch) lengths
3 tbs oil

For a rich flavour, the chicken should be marinated for a couple of hours. Put it in a shallow glass or ceramic dish. Combine the soy sauce, mirin, sherry, brown sugar and ginger and stir until the sugar dissolves. Pour the marinade over the chicken, give a good stir, then cover with plastic wrap and refrigerate for a couple of hours, turning every so often.

If you're using bamboo skewers, avoid a fiery accident by soaking them in water for at least 30 minutes before using. Prepare and oil the grill (broiler). Lift the chicken out of the marinade, then cut the tenderloins in half lengthways.

The chicken now gets threaded onto the skewers, with a piece capsicum and spring onion between each chicken bit. Brush the kebabs with oil and grill under medium heat until the chicken is tender, about 7 minutes. While they're cooking, brush them with oil and turn them over occasionally. Serve with mounds of rice.
Makes 12.

Teriyaki is a Japanese term referring to meat or fish that has been marinated in soy sauce, skewered, then grilled.

To allow the flavours in the meat sauce to fully infuse, make it a day in advance and refrigerate overnight. Then it's simply a question of whipping up the cheese sauce, assembling the moussaka, and imagining that you're dining on a Greek isle.

moussaka

3 eggplants (aubergines), cut into
1 cm (1/2 inch) slices
125 ml (1/2 cup) olive oil

For the filling:
2 tbs olive oil
1 large onion, finely chopped
500 g (1 lb 2 oz) minced (ground) lean beef
2 tbs dry white wine
425 g (15 oz) can chopped tomatoes
1 tbs finely chopped flat-leaf (Italian) parsley
2 tsp finely chopped mint leaves
1/2 tsp ground cinnamon

For the cheese sauce:
90 g (31/4 oz) butter
4 tbs plain (all-purpose) flour
500 ml (2 cups) milk
2 eggs, lightly beaten
85 g (2/3 cup) grated Parmesan cheese

First remove any bitterness from the eggplant by sprinkling it with salt and draining in a colander for an hour. Then rinse, drain and squeeze. Fry a few pieces at a time in the oil until golden, then drain on paper towels.

To make the filling, cook the onion and beef in the hot oil in a frying pan until the meat browns. Now add the wine, tomato, herbs and cinnamon and bring to the boil. Reduce to a simmer, then put the lid on and simmer for 20 minutes, stirring occasionally. Take off the lid and bubble away for 10 minutes more.

For the cheese sauce, heat the butter in a small pan over low heat until it starts to foam, then add the flour and stir for 2 minutes. Slowly pour in the milk, stirring at the same time, until you have a smooth sauce. Increase the heat a little and stir until it boils and thickens, about 5 minutes. Cook for a minute, then take off the hob and beat in the eggs and cheese.

To assemble the moussaka, layer the eggplant and filling — starting and finishing with the eggplant. For the final touch, spread cheese sauce over the top, then bake for 45 minutes in a 180°C (350°F/Gas 4) oven until golden. Serves 6.

duck a l'orange

5 oranges, 2 halved,
the rest zested and juiced
2 kg (4¹/2 lb) duck
2 cinnamon sticks
15 g (³/4 cup) mint leaves
4 tbs soft brown sugar
125 ml (¹/2 cup) cider vinegar
4 tbs Grand Marnier
30 g (1 oz) butter

Massage the orange halves into the duck, then push them into the duck cavity with the cinnamon sticks and mint. Tie the legs together and tie the wings together. Prick all over with a fork. Put the duck on a rack, breast-side down, in a shallow roasting tin. Roast for 45 minutes in a 150°C (300°F/Gas 2) oven, turning the duck halfway through.

Meanwhile, heat the sugar in a saucepan over low heat until it melts and then caramelizes, swirling the pan gently. Add the vinegar and boil for 3 minutes. Pour in the orange juice and Grand Marnier and simmer for 2 minutes. Blanch the orange zest in boiling water three times, changing the water each time. Refresh under cold water, drain and reserve.

Scoop out the excess fat from the tin. Increase the heat to 180°C (350°F/Gas 4). Spoon some of the orange sauce over the duck and roast for 45 minutes, spooning sauce over the duck every 10 minutes and turning the duck. Take it out of the oven, cover with foil and strain the juices into a saucepan. Skim off any excess fat and add the orange zest and butter to the saucepan. Now stir until the butter melts and the sauce is hot. Drizzle over the duck. Serves 4.

It's easy to see why this was once the star of the menu in any restaurant worthy of its trade. Now's the time to rediscover it for yourself.

Essentially a béchamel sauce that's flavoured with cheese, mornay goes beautifully with eggs or an assortment of vegetables if you don't want to limit it to fish.

tuna mornay

60 g (2¼ oz) butter
2 tbs plain (all-purpose) flour
500 ml (2 cups) milk
½ tsp dry mustard
90 g (¾ cup) grated Cheddar cheese
600 g (1 lb 5 oz) canned tuna
in brine, drained
2 tbs finely chopped parsley
2 eggs, hard-boiled and chopped
4 tbs fresh breadcrumbs
paprika

Begin with the sauce — melt the butter in a small saucepan, add the flour and stir over low heat for 1 minute. Take the pan off the hob and slowly pour in the milk, stirring with your other hand until you have a smooth sauce. Return the pan to the heat and stir constantly until the sauce boils and thickens. Reduce the heat and simmer for another 2 minutes. Once again, take the pan off the heat, this time to whisk in the mustard and two-thirds of the cheese — don't stop whisking until you have a smooth, rich cheesy sauce.

Roughly flake the tuna with a fork, then tip it into the cheesy sauce, along with the parsley and egg. Season with a little salt and pepper, then spoon the mixture into four 250 ml (1 cup) ovenproof ramekins.

Make the topping by mixing together the breadcrumbs and the rest of the cheese, then sprinkle it over the mornay. Add a hint of colour by dusting the top very lightly with paprika. Pop in a 180°C (350°F/Gas 4) oven until the topping is golden brown, about 20 minutes.
Serves 4.

spaghetti with meatballs

For the meatballs:
500 g (1 lb 2 oz) minced (ground) beef
40 g (¹/2 cup) fresh breadcrumbs
1 onion, finely chopped
2 garlic cloves, crushed
2 tsp Worcestershire sauce
1 tsp dried oregano
3 tbs plain (all-purpose) flour
2 tbs olive oil

For the sauce:
2 x 425 g (15 oz) cans chopped tomatoes
1 onion, finely chopped
1 tbs olive oil
2 garlic cloves, crushed
2 tbs tomato paste (purée)
125 ml (¹/2 cup) beef stock
2 tsp sugar

500 g (1 lb 2 oz) spaghetti
grated Parmesan cheese

To make the meatball mixture, combine the beef, breadcrumbs, onion, garlic, Worcestershire sauce, oregano and some salt and pepper in a bowl. Don't be squeamish — get your hands in there and mix it all up. Now roll the mixture into meatballs, using about a tablespoon of mixture for each one. Lightly dust the meatballs with flour and shake off the excess before frying them in the hot oil in batches, turning frequently, until browned all over. Drain them well on paper towels.

To make the sauce, blitz the tomatoes in a food processor or blender until puréed. Fry the onion in the oil over medium heat for a few minutes until soft and lightly golden, before adding the garlic and cooking for just a minute more. Stir in the puréed tomatoes, tomato paste, stock and sugar, then let the sauce come to the boil. Add the meatballs to the bubbling sauce, then reduce the heat and simmer for 15 minutes, turning the meatballs once. Season with salt and pepper.

Meanwhile, cook the spaghetti in a large pan of boiling water until *al dente*. Drain, then pile some on four serving plates. Top with the meatballs and sauce and a little Parmesan. Serves 4.

A favourite with children who love chasing the little meatballs around the plate ... why not join them?

Often associated with school lunches, this nourishing dish is something you'll never outgrow. (Hopefully food fights are a thing of the past, though.)

silverside and parsley sauce

1.5 kg (3 lb 5 oz) corned silverside
1 tsp black peppercorns
5 cloves
2 bay leaves, torn
2 tbs soft brown sugar

For the parsley sauce:
50 g (1³/4 oz) butter
1¹/2 tbs plain (all-purpose) flour
400 ml (14 fl oz) milk
125 ml (¹/2 cup) beef stock
2 tbs chopped parsley

Soak the corned beef in cold water for 45 minutes, changing the water 3–4 times. This helps eliminate some of the salty flavour.

Lift the beef out of the water and put it in a large heavy-based saucepan with the peppercorns, cloves, bay leaves, brown sugar and enough cold water to just cover it. Bring to the boil, then reduce the heat to very low and simmer for 1¹/2–1³/4 hours. Turn the meat over every half hour and keep an eye on the water level — you'll probably need to add some more. You don't want the water to boil or the meat will become tough, so use a heat diffuser mat if you need to. Remove the meat from the pan and let it rest for 15 minutes.

To make the parsley sauce, melt the butter in a saucepan over medium heat and then stir in the flour and keep stirring for 1 minute. Take the pan off the hob and pour in the milk and stock, whisking until smooth. Return the pan to the heat and cook, whisking constantly, until the sauce boils and thickens. Reduce the heat and simmer for 2 minutes more before stirring in the parsley and a little salt and pepper. Serve over slices of silverside with steamed vegetables.
Serves 6.

beef carbonnade

30 g (1 oz) butter
2–3 tbs oil
1 kg (2 lb 4 oz) lean beef rump or
chuck steak, cubed
4 onions, chopped
1 garlic clove, crushed
1 tsp brown sugar
1 tbs plain (all-purpose) flour
500 ml (2 cups) beer (bitter or stout)
2 bay leaves
4 sprigs of thyme

For the croûtons:
6–8 slices baguette
Dijon mustard

Melt the butter in a large frying pan with a tablespoon of oil. Brown the meat in batches over high heat and then lift out onto a plate.

Add a tablespoon of oil and the onion to the pan. Cook over moderate heat for 10 minutes, then add the garlic and sugar and cook for a further 5 minutes, adding a little more oil if necessary. Put the onion onto a second plate.

Reduce the heat to low and pour in any juices that have drained from the meat, then stir in the flour. Remove from the heat and stir in the beer, a little at a time (it will foam). Return to the heat and simmer and thicken. Season.

Layer the meat and onion in a casserole dish, tucking the bay leaves and sprigs of thyme between the layers and seasoning as you go. Pour the liquid over the meat, cover with a lid and cook in a 150°C (300°F/Gas 2) oven for 2¹/2–3 hours, or until the meat is tender.

To make the croûtons, preheat the grill. Lightly toast the baguette on both sides, then spread one side with mustard. Arrange on top of the carbonnade, mustard-side up, and stick the whole casserole under the grill for a minute. Serves 4.

There's something so hale and hearty about a recipe that combines beer and beef, probably because you can satisfy your hunger and slake your thirst in one glorious mouthful.

Pour yourself a glass of red from the bottle you're cooking with — if it's good enough to drink, then it's good enough for cooking.

boeuf bourguignon

2 tbs olive oil
1 kg (2 lb 4 oz) trimmed chuck steak, cubed
12 baby onions, halved, with the
root base left intact
4 bacon rashers, chopped
2 garlic cloves, finely chopped
3 tbs plain (all-purpose) flour
375 ml (1¹/2 cups) red wine
2 bay leaves
5 sprigs of parsley
3 sprigs of thyme
1 thin slice of lemon zest
375 ml (1¹/2 cups) beef or chicken stock
500 g (1 lb 2 oz) flat mushrooms, halved

Heat half the oil in a large heavy-based pan, then brown the meat in small batches. Lift the meat out onto a plate.

Now heat the rest of the oil in the same pan over medium heat and use it to cook the onion, bacon and garlic until the onion is browned, about 5 minutes. Return the beef to the pan, add the flour, and stir for a minute. Lift the pan off the heat, and gradually stir in the wine, mixing the flour in well. Return the pan to the heat and bring to the boil, stirring, then reduce the heat and simmer for 3 minutes, or until the sauce boils and thickens slightly.

Make a bouquet garni by wrapping the bay leaves, parsley, thyme and lemon zest in a piece of muslin and tying with string. Add the bouquet garni, stock and mushrooms to the pan and bring to the boil. For the last stage, reduce the heat to low so that the liquid is simmering gently, pop on the lid and leave it alone for 2 hours except for the occasional stir. By this stage the beef should be tender. Fish out the bouquet garni, taste for seasoning, then dollop generous portions onto plates with mash to soak up the juices. Serves 4.

beef pot roast

300 g (10$\frac{1}{2}$ oz) baby onions
40 g (1$\frac{1}{2}$ oz) butter
2 carrots, cut into bite-size chunks
3 parsnips, cut into bite-size chunks
1–1.5 kg (2 lb 4 oz–3 lb 5 oz) piece of silverside, trimmed
3 tbs dry red wine
1 large tomato, finely chopped
250 ml (1 cup) beef stock

Cover the onions with boiling water for about a minute, then drain. Cool, then slip off the skins.

Heat half the butter in a large heavy-based pan that will tightly fit the meat (it will shrink during cooking), add the onions, carrots and parsnips and cook, stirring, over medium heat until browned. Remove the vegetables, then add the remaining butter to the pan and use it to brown the meat all over. Next, pour in the wine, bring to the boil, then add the tomato and stock. Return to the boil, then reduce the heat to low, put the lid on and leave to gently simmer for 2 hours, turning only once. After this time, add the vegetables and simmer for another hour.

Lift the meat out onto a carving board. Cover with foil and rest while finishing the sauce.

Increase the heat to high and boil the pan juices with the vegetables for 10 minutes to reduce and slightly thicken the sauce. Skim off any excess fat, and taste before seasoning. Slice the meat and arrange on a serving platter with the vegetables. Drizzle with the pan juices and serve.
Serves 6.

We love these easy all-in-one meals that leave you plenty of time to get on with the important things in life.

If you harbour the desire to dine like a king, even for just a day, then hurry down to the local fish markets and treat yourself to one of nature's richest treasures from the ocean's depths.

lobster mornay

1 cooked lobster
315 ml (1¼ cups) milk
1 slice of onion
1 bay leaf
6 black peppercorns
30 g (1 oz) butter
2 tbs plain (all-purpose) flour
pinch of freshly grated nutmeg
2 tbs cream
60 g (½ cup) grated Cheddar cheese

The lobster can be a bit tricky to prepare, but if you have a sharp knife and lobster crackers, you're halfway there. First cut the lobster in half lengthways, then lift the meat from the tail and body of the lobster. Crack the legs and prise the meat from them. Remove the intestinal vein and soft body matter and discard. Cut the meat into 2 cm (3/4 inch) pieces, cover and refrigerate. Wash the shell halves, drain, dry and keep until needed.

Now for the mornay sauce: heat the milk in a small saucepan with the onion, bay leaf and peppercorns. Bring to the boil and then take the pan off the hob, put the lid on and let the flavours infuse into the milk for 15 minutes. Strain. Melt the butter in a large saucepan, add the flour and stir for 1 minute. Remove from the heat, then gradually pour in the milk, whisking with your other hand. Return to the hob and keep whisking over medium heat until the mixture boils and thickens. Season with salt, pepper and nutmeg. Stir in the cream.

Fold the lobster meat through the rich sauce, then artistically arrange the mixture in the lobster shells. Sprinkle the top with cheese and melt the cheese under a preheated grill. Serves 2.

fettucine carbonara

500 g (1 lb 2 oz) fettucine
3 eggs, lightly beaten
125 ml (1/2 cup) whipping cream
4 tbs finely grated Parmesan cheese
15 g (1/2 oz) butter
250 g (9 oz) bacon, cut into thin strips
2 garlic cloves, crushed

First of all, cook the fettucine in a large saucepan of boiling water until *al dente*.

Meanwhile, whisk together the eggs, cream and Parmesan and a generous amount of salt and freshly ground black pepper.

Melt the butter in a frying pan, add the bacon strips and cook until lightly golden. Add the garlic and cook for 1–2 minutes more before taking the pan off the heat.

The idea with this meal is that the heat of the pasta will cook the sauce. So, as soon as the pasta is cooked, drain it, then lift it into a serving bowl. Pour in the egg mixture and toss thoroughly until the strands of fettucine are glistening. Add the bacon mixture and again toss the pasta. Season to taste with freshly ground black pepper and serve. Serves 4.

According to film director Federico Fellini, 'Life is a combination of magic and pasta'. Or in the case of this magical creation, cream and pasta.

The ingredients for chicken cacciatore, once the meal of the hunter, can now easily be picked up by gatherers at the local shop.

chicken cacciatore

3 tbs olive oil
1 large onion, finely chopped
3 garlic cloves, crushed
1 celery stalk, finely chopped
150 g (5$\frac{1}{2}$ oz) pancetta, finely chopped
125 g (4$\frac{1}{2}$ oz) button mushrooms, thickly sliced
4 chicken drumsticks
4 chicken thighs
4 tbs dry vermouth or dry white wine
2 x 400 g (14 oz) cans chopped tomatoes
$\frac{1}{4}$ tsp brown sugar
1 sprig of rosemary
1 bay leaf
a few sprigs of oregano

Heat half the oil in a large casserole dish. Add the onion, garlic and celery and cook, stirring from time to time, until the onion is golden — it should take about 7 minutes. Add the pancetta and mushrooms, increase the heat and cook, stirring occasionally, for 5 minutes. Lift out onto a plate.

Add the remaining oil to the casserole and lightly brown the chicken pieces, a few at a time, then season with salt and pepper. Spoon off any excess fat and return all the pieces to the casserole. Splash in the vermouth, increase the heat and cook until the liquid has almost evaporated.

Add the tomato, sugar, rosemary, bay leaf, a sprig of oregano and 4 tablespoons water. Bring to the boil then stir in the reserved pancetta mixture. Now put the lid on and simmer for 20 minutes until the chicken is tender but not falling off the bone. If the liquid is too thin, remove the chicken from the casserole, increase the heat and boil until thickened. Discard the sprigs of herbs and taste for salt and pepper. Serve with a garnish of oregano.
Serves 4.

shepherd's pie

1 kg (2 lb 4 oz) potatoes, peeled and
cut into chunks
30 g (1 oz) butter
2 tbs milk
1 large onion, finely chopped
1 tbs oil
1 kg (2 lb 4 oz) minced (ground) lamb
1 carrot, finely chopped
2 tbs plain (all-purpose) flour
250 ml (1 cup) vegetable stock
2 tbs Worcestershire sauce
155 g (1 cup) frozen peas

First, cook the potato in a large saucepan of boiling water until tender, about 20 minutes. Then, drain well and return the potato to the pan for another minute or so over low heat to evaporate all the water. Remove the pan from the heat, add the butter and milk, and mash until smooth and fluffy. Season to taste.

While the potato is cooking, fry the onion in oil in a large frying pan until soft and just beginning to colour. Add the mince, increase the heat and cook until browned. If there are any lumps, break them up with a wooden spoon. Add the carrot and cook for a few minutes until just tender, then sprinkle with flour and cook, stirring, for 1 minute. Slowly pour in the stock, stirring constantly at the same time. Once all the stock has been added, splash in the Worcestershire sauce and boil until the gravy thickens — 2 minutes should do it. Season, then throw in the peas.

Scoop the whole lot into a 2 litre (8 cup) ovenproof dish. Spoon the mashed potato over the top and spread out evenly. Create gorgeous swirls and curls with a fork. Bake for about 45 minutes in a 180°C (350°F/Gas 4) oven until the potato is golden.
Serves 6.

Made with lamb, it's known as shepherd's pie, with beef, as cottage pie. Either way, it's certain to bring the herd home in time for dinner.

Not even the KGB could prevent one of Russia's top-secret recipes being smuggled out of the country. Serve it with a shot of vodka for an authentic experience.

beef stroganoff

2 tbs plain (all-purpose) flour
500 g (1 lb 2 oz) rump steak, trimmed and
thinly sliced across the grain
2 tbs olive oil
1 onion, finely chopped
1 garlic clove, crushed
400 g (14 oz) button mushrooms, sliced
1 tbs tomato paste (purée)
300 g (10 1/2 oz) sour cream
finely chopped parsley

The beef needs to be coated in flour. An easy way to do this is to put the flour and some salt and pepper in a plastic bag with the steak. Now shake vigorously until it's covered in flour. Shake off any excess flour.

Heat half the oil in a heavy-based frying pan over high heat, then cook the meat until nicely browned — do this in batches to prevent the meat from stewing. Lift the meat out onto a plate.

Heat the remaining oil in the pan and add the onion. Cook until soft and translucent, about 2 minutes, then add the garlic and stir briefly. Next add the mushrooms and cook them until they soften, about 3 minutes. Stir in the tomato paste and sour cream, then return the beef strips to the pan. Keep over the heat just until the meat is warmed through, then sprinkle with chopped parsley before serving. Great with mounds of rice. Serves 4.

coq au vin

1 tbs olive oil
12 baby onions, peeled
3 bacon rashers, chopped
40 g (1½ oz) butter
1.5 kg (3 lb 5 oz) chicken pieces
2 garlic cloves, crushed
375 ml (1½ cups) red wine
1 tbs chopped thyme
1 bay leaf
4 parsley stalks
250 g (9 oz) button mushrooms, halved
25 g (1 oz) butter, extra, softened
1 tbs plain (all-purpose) flour
chopped parsley

In a hot frying pan, brown the onions in the oil, shaking the pan occasionally. Add the bacon and brown it too. Lift the onions and bacon onto a plate (use a slotted spoon for this), then add the butter to the pan. When it's foaming, fry the chicken in batches until golden, then lift out into an ovenproof dish. Add the onions and bacon to the dish.

Tip any excess fat out of the frying pan and add the garlic, wine, thyme, bay leaf and parsley stalks. Bring to the boil, then pour over the chicken. Cover the dish and bake in a 170°C (325°F/Gas 3) oven for 1½ hours, before adding the mushrooms and cooking for another half hour — by this stage the mushrooms should be tender. Drain the liquid into a pan. Keep the chicken and other solids warm in the oven (except for the bay leaf and parsley, which can be discarded).

Make a sort of paste with the softened butter and flour. Bring the liquid in the pan to the boil, then whisk in the buttery paste in two batches. Reduce the heat and simmer until the liquid thickens slightly. Serve up the chicken, splash on some sauce, scatter with parsley, then serve.
Serves 4.

If you have a hankering for those large, plump, tasty birds you remember from childhood, be sure to buy free-range chickens.

For those who like an extra rich, thick goulash, take the lid off and cook over high heat for five minutes before you add the sour cream.

veal goulash

500 g (1 lb 2 oz) veal, cut into
2.5 cm (1 inch) pieces
2 tbs plain (all-purpose) flour
2 tbs olive oil
2 onions, thinly sliced
2 garlic cloves, finely chopped
1 tbs sweet Hungarian paprika
1 tsp ground cumin
425 g (15 oz) can chopped tomatoes
2 carrots, sliced
half a red capsicum (pepper), chopped
half a green capsicum (pepper), chopped
250 ml (1 cup) beef stock
125 ml ($1/2$ cup) red wine
125 g ($1/2$ cup) sour cream
chopped parsley

Put the veal and flour in a plastic bag and give a good shake until the veal is evenly coated. When you're done, shake off any excess. Heat 1 tablespoon oil in a large, deep pan over medium heat, then brown the meat in batches, before lifting out onto a plate.

Add the remaining oil to the pan. Cook the onion, garlic, paprika and cumin for 5 minutes, stirring frequently. Return the meat and any juices to the pan with the tomato, carrot and capsicums. Put the lid on and cook for 10 minutes.

Pour in the stock and wine and season with salt and pepper. Stir well, then put the lid on and simmer over very low heat for 1$1/2$ hours. Now stir in half the sour cream, season with more salt and pepper if needed and serve garnished with parsley and the remaining sour cream. Delicious served with buttery boiled small potatoes or noodles.
Serves 4.

tournedos sautés chasseur

90 g (3¼ oz) butter
1 garlic clove, crushed
4 slices of bread
1 tbs oil
4 fillet steaks, each 3 cm (1¼ inches) thick, patted dry
4 finely chopped shallots
200 g (7 oz) button mushrooms, halved
170 ml (⅔ cup) beef stock
2 tsp tomato paste (purée)
3 tbs dry Madeira or white wine
2 tsp cornflour (cornstarch)
2 tbs chopped parsley

Make a fragrant garlicky butter by melting a third of the butter in a small pan with the garlic. Cut the bread into rounds the same size as the steaks. Lightly brush both sides of the bread rounds with the garlic butter before toasting on a baking tray in a 180°C (350°F/ Gas 4) oven until golden, about 20 minutes.

At the same time, heat the oil and half the remaining butter in a frying pan. Cook the steaks over high heat for 3–7 minutes each side, depending on how you like your steak. Lift them out onto a warm plate.

Heat the rest of the butter in the pan, add the shallots and cook for 2 minutes before adding the mushrooms and cooking for another 5 minutes. Season well, then remove from the pan. Add the stock and tomato paste to the pan and boil rapidly until reduced to about 4 tablespoons. Make a paste out of the Madeira and cornflour, then add to the pan and bring to the boil, stirring, until it thickens a little. Return the mushrooms and shallots to the pan along with the parsley.

Sit each steak on a toasted bread round, with a generous amount of sauce.
Serves 4.

Any dish designated 'chasseur' or 'hunter', would have originally been made with game meat. Today, it's perfectly sporting to use the term in regard to any sort of meat.

Named in honour of the Duke of Wellington after the Battle of Waterloo, 'tis a noble dish to set before your weary troops … or simply an army of famished friends.

beef wellington

1.25 kg (2 lb 12 oz) piece of beef fillet or
rib eye, trimmed
1 tbs oil
125 g (4¹/₂ oz) pâté
60 g (2¹/₄ oz) button mushrooms, sliced
375 g (13 oz) block of puff pastry, thawed
1 egg, lightly beaten
1 sheet ready-rolled puff pastry, thawed

To help the beef keep its shape, tie it four or five times along its length, then rub with pepper. Heat the oil over high heat in a large, heavy-based pan, then cook the meat until it's browned all over. Take the beef out of the pan and let it cool, then cut off the string. Smear the pâté over the top and sides of the beef, then use this as glue for the mushrooms.

The idea is to enclose the beef in pastry. So start by rolling the block of pastry out on a lightly floured surface until it's big enough. Then sit the beef on the pastry, brush the edges with egg and bring the edges up until you have a parcel of beef. Use some more of the beaten egg to seal the parcel, then neatly fold in the ends. Lift the beef onto a greased baking tray so the seam is underneath.

Now for the decoration — cut shapes from the puff pastry. Use the egg to stick the shapes on, then brush all over the Wellington with more of the egg. Cut a few slits in the top to allow the steam to escape. Cook in a 210°C (415°F/Gas 6–7) oven for 45 minutes for rare, 1 hour for medium or 1¹/₂ hours for well done (cover with foil if the pastry is browning too much). Rest for 10 minutes, the slice and serve. Serves 6–8.

glazed ham

7 kg (15 lb 4 oz) leg ham
1 large orange, peeled, with the zest
cut into long thin strips, and
125 ml (1/2 cup) juice squeezed
cloves
140 g (3/4 cup) soft brown sugar
1 tbs Dijon mustard
175 g (1/2 cup) honey
2 tsp soy sauce
2 tbs Grand Marnier

Cut through the ham rind around the shank end and start to peel back the rind, lifting it up by pushing your thumb under the edge. Carefully peel the whole thing off. Sit the ham on a rack in a deep roasting tin. Add 500 ml (2 cups) water, the zest and 6 cloves to the dish. Cover tightly with foil, and cook for 2 hours in a 180°C (350°F/Gas 4) oven, then take out of the oven. Increase the heat to 210°C (415°F/Gas 6–7). Drain the meat and reserve 250 ml (1 cup) of the pan juices. Now score a diamond pattern into the ham fat.

Combine the sugar, mustard, honey, soy sauce and Grand Marnier. Brush some of this glaze over the ham, then return the ham to the oven and cook, uncovered, for 30 minutes, brushing with glaze every 10 minutes. Take the ham out of the oven and press a clove into each diamond. Roast, uncovered, for another hour, brushing with the glaze every 10 minutes.

Pour the reserved pan juices and 125 ml (1/2 cup) of the glaze into a small saucepan and pour in the reserved orange juice. Stir over low heat until the mixture boils, then boil, without stirring, for 3 minutes. Rest the ham for 10 minutes before serving with the glaze. Serves 20.

Don't save a cooked ham until Christmas — it's something that can be enjoyed all year round and is particularly good at buffets or large gatherings.

something on the side

An old Irish saying states that there are only two things in life too important to joke about — potatoes and matrimony. So how about this for a seriously good recipe?

potato salad

600 g (1 lb 5 oz) waxy potatoes, unpeeled
and cut into bite-size pieces
1 small onion, finely chopped
1 small green capsicum (pepper), chopped
2–3 celery stalks, chopped
3 tbs finely chopped parsley

For the dressing:
185 g (3/4 cup) whole-egg mayonnaise
1–2 tbs white wine vinegar or lemon juice
2 tbs sour cream

The first step is to cook the potatoes until the flesh is tender, but watch them carefully so the skins don't break away. Either boil or steam them for 5–10 minutes, then drain and let cool completely.

Combine the onion, capsicum, celery and most of the parsley with the potato in a large bowl — keep the rest of the parsley aside for a garnish.

To make the dressing, mix together all the ingredients into a thick, creamy mixture and add a little salt and pepper. Dollop over the salad and toss gently until the potato is coated. Garnish with the reserved parsley, then serve.
Serves 4.

sautéed potatoes

1 kg (2 lb 4 oz) all-purpose potatoes, peeled
and cut into 2 cm (3/4 inch) cubes
4 tbs olive oil
1 garlic clove, crushed

Steam or boil the potatoes for 5 minutes. Drain well, then dab them with a clean tea towel so they're really dry.

Get a large frying pan with a lid, then heat the oil in the pan (you won't need the lid just yet). Add the potato and cook over low heat for about 10 minutes, stirring frequently so that the potato doesn't stick to the bottom. Put the lid on and cook for 10 minutes more, giving the pan a good shake every now and then — the steam will help cook the potato.

Add the garlic and some salt and black pepper in the last few minutes of cooking. If at the end of the cooking time the potatoes aren't looking as crisp as you'd like, blast them over high heat for a minute or so. Serves 4–6.

If you're preparing for a dinner party, the potatoes can be cooked ahead of time and reheated in a heavy-based pan brushed with olive oil.

Probably one of the most popular ways of eating cabbage — even children love this mixture of vegetables in creamy mayonnaise. Perfect for picnics.

coleslaw

half of a green cabbage
quarter of a red cabbage
3 carrots, coarsely grated
6 radishes, coarsely grated
1 red capsicum (pepper), chopped
4 spring onions (scallions), sliced
3 tbs chopped parsley
250 g (1 cup) whole-egg mayonnaise

The first step is to get rid of the hard central core from the cabbages. Once that is done, shred the leaves with a sharp knife. Tumble all the shredded leaves into a large bowl, then add the carrot, radish, capsicum, spring onion and parsley.

Add the mayonnaise, season to taste with salt and freshly ground black pepper, then toss vigorously until it's all mixed together. Serves 8–10.

To save time, you can cover and refrigerate the chopped vegetables for up to 3 hours before serving. Add the mayonnaise just before serving.

croquettes

750 g (1 lb 10 oz) floury potatoes,
peeled and quartered
2 tbs cream or melted butter
3 eggs, 2 of them lightly beaten
1/4 tsp freshly grated nutmeg
plain (all-purpose) flour
150 g (1 1/2 cups) dry breadcrumbs
oil, for deep-frying

Cook the potatoes for 10–15 minutes until just tender — you can either boil or steam them. Drain well, then put them back in their pan over the heat just until all the moisture evaporates. Use your potato masher or a fork to mash the potato into fluffy clouds. Stir in the cream or melted butter, one egg, the nutmeg and some salt and freshly ground black pepper until it's smooth and combined. Spread the potato onto a plate with a wooden spoon, cover with plastic wrap and refrigerate for at least 30 minutes.

Divide the potato mixture into 12 portions, then roll each one into a fat, round finger. Roll each finger first in the flour (shake off the excess), then dip in the beaten egg, then coat evenly in the crumbs. Lay the crumbed croquettes out on a tray or plate, cover with plastic wrap and refrigerate for at least 2 hours.

Deep-fry the croquettes in batches for 5 minutes until hot, golden and crisp. Remove carefully with a slotted spoon, drain on paper towels and keep warm while you cook the rest of them.
Makes 12.

The combination of fluffy potato beneath a crunchy golden skin is irresistible.

Some foods were created purely to give you the opportunity to throw away the calorie counter and indulge yourself.

munchy potato skins with guacamole

1.5 kg (3 lb 5 oz) floury or all-purpose potatoes, unpeeled
oil, for deep-frying

For the guacamole:
2 ripe avocados
1 small tomato, finely chopped
1 small red onion, finely chopped
2–3 tbs sour cream
1 tbs lime juice
1 tbs chopped coriander (cilantro)
2–3 drops of Tabasco sauce

First scrub the potatoes clean, then dry them in a clean tea towel — they need to be as dry as possible. Prick the potatoes a couple of times with a fork, then put them on a baking tray and bake for 1 hour in a 210°C (415°F/Gas 6–7) oven, turning once, until the skins are crisp and the flesh is soft. They need to be cool, so set them aside for an hour.

While the potato is cooling, move onto the guacamole: mash the avocado flesh in a bowl, then mix in everything else and a touch of salt and black pepper.

When the potatoes are cool, cut them in half lengthways and scoop out most of the flesh, leaving 1 cm ($1/2$ inch) of potato in the skin. To make the wedges, cut each half in three, again cutting lengthways.

Deep-fry the potato skins in batches for 2–3 minutes, or until dark golden and crisp. Remove with a slotted spoon and drain on paper towels. Salt them enthusiastically and serve with the guacamole.
Serves 4–6.

vichy carrots

800 g (1 lb 12 oz) carrots
1½ tsp sugar
50 g (1¾ oz) butter
1½ tbs chopped parsley

Slice the carrots into thin rounds, then put them in a deep frying pan. Just cover with cold water and add the sugar, butter and ½ teaspoon salt. Cover and simmer over low heat until the carrots are nearly tender, then remove the lid and boil until any remaining liquid evaporates. Serve sprinkled with finely chopped parsley and small knobs of butter. Serves 6.

After a decade of 90s minimalism, it's time to dress up your vegetables in their tastiest attire.

Given that just about every nationality eats potatoes in one form or another, it's not surprising there are so many different ways to serve them. Here's a particularly luscious play on the humble spud.

duchess potatoes

1 kg (2 lb 4 oz) floury potatoes,
peeled and quartered
2 eggs
4 tbs whipping cream
1/4 tsp freshly grated nutmeg
1 egg yolk

Before the potatoes are baked, they need to be cooked until tender. You can either steam or boil them — about 12 minutes should be long enough. Next, drain them, then put them back in their pan over the heat until any remaining moisture evaporates, then mash into fluffy clouds.

Beat together the whole eggs, cream, nutmeg and some salt and black pepper. Pour the whole lot in with the potato and mash until you have a smooth, reasonably thick mash. Keep in mind that the mixture will have to be piped, so you might need to add a little extra cream if your mixture is too thick. Let the mash cool slightly.

Spoon the potato into a piping bag with a 1.5 cm (5/8 inch) star nozzle. Pipe pretty swirls onto two baking trays, leaving some space between each one. Brush with the yolk so they will turn golden, then bake in a 180°C (350°F/Gas 4) oven for about 15 minutes. Serves 6.

rosti

750 g (1 lb 10 oz) waxy or all-purpose
potatoes, unpeeled
60 g (2¼ oz) butter

The first step is to cook the potatoes until just tender, about 15 minutes will do. Drain, then leave to cool. When they are cool enough to touch, peel off and throw away the skins. Now leave them cool to room temperature.

Now grate the potatoes on the coarse side of the grater, then add some salt and pepper to the mountain of potato. Heat 40 g (1½ oz) of the butter in a 20 cm (8 inch) heavy-based frying pan. When the butter starts to fizz, add the grated potato and press down gently to form a potato pancake.

Cook the rosti over medium heat until the bottom is crisp, crusty and golden brown, but not burnt. Shake the pan occasionally to prevent the potato sticking. The easiest way to get the rosti out of the pan is to hold a large plate over the frying pan and tip the frying pan upside down.

Heat the remaining butter in the same pan, then slide the rosti back into the pan. Cook for a further 15–20 minutes, or until the bottom is also crisp and golden. Serve piping hot, cut into wedges.
Serves 4.

These Swiss-style potatoes can be flavoured with onion or bacon for additional appeal.

Such a scrumptious way to get children (and adults) to eat their cauliflower and ask for more.

cauliflower cheese

500 g (1 lb 2 oz) cauliflower, cut into florets
30 g (1 oz) butter
3 tbs plain (all-purpose) flour
315 ml (1¼ cups) warm milk
1 tsp Dijon mustard
60 g (½ cup) grated Cheddar cheese
50 g (½ cup) grated Parmesan cheese
2 tbs fresh breadcrumbs
3 tbs grated Cheddar cheese, extra

First cook the cauliflower florets in lightly salted boiling water until just tender. Drain, then tumble into a greased 1.5 litre (6 cup) heatproof dish and keep warm.

Melt the butter in a saucepan. Stir in the flour and cook for 1–2 minutes until golden and bubbling. Take the pan off the heat and slowly whisk in the milk and mustard. Return to the heat and bring to the boil, stirring constantly. Lower the heat and simmer until you have a smooth sauce that coats the spoon — 2 minutes should do the trick. Once more, remove the pan from the heat, this time to stir in the cheeses until they melt. Don't reheat the sauce or you'll end up with an oily slick. Season with salt and white pepper and then ooze the sauce all over the cauliflower.

Crumble together the breadcrumbs and extra cheese and sprinkle over the top. Grill until the top is browned and bubbling, then serve while deliciously hot.
Serves 4.

dauphinoise

25 g (1 oz) butter
1 onion, halved and thinly sliced
650 g (1 lb 7 oz) floury potatoes, peeled
and thinly sliced
85 g (2/3 cup) grated Cheddar cheese
300 ml (10 1/2 fl oz) whipping cream
100 ml (3 1/2 fl oz) milk

Heat the butter in a frying pan and cook the onion over low heat until it is soft and translucent, about 5 minutes.

Layer the potato slices, onion and most of the cheese (keep a little aside to sprinkle over the top) in a lightly greased 1 litre (4 cup) ovenproof dish. Whisk together the cream and milk, and season with salt and pepper. Slowly pour over the potato, then sprinkle with the remaining cheese.

Bake for about an hour in a 160°C (315°F/ Gas 2–3) oven until soft and golden brown on the top. Leave for 10 minutes before serving. Serves 4.

Rub the gratin dish with a clove of cut garlic before you butter it to give your potatoes an extra element of flavour.

midnight suppers

You'll never be tempted to buy another sausage roll once you've tried these delicious homemade ones.

classic sausage rolls

150 g (5½ oz) minced (ground) sausage
150 g (5½ oz) minced (ground) lean beef
1 small onion, finely chopped or grated
1–2 garlic cloves, crushed
1 tbs tomato sauce
3 tsp Worcestershire sauce
40 g (½ cup) fresh breadcrumbs
2–3 tbs finely chopped parsley
2 eggs
2 sheets ready-rolled puff pastry

Line two baking trays with baking paper. For the filling, get a large bowl and put in it the meats, onion, garlic, sauces, breadcrumbs, parsley, one of the eggs and some salt and pepper, then get your hands in there and mix it all together.

Cut the pastry sheets in half and brush them lightly with some of the remaining beaten egg. Divide the filling mixture into four equal portions and roll each portion into a sausage long enough to lay on the middle of each pastry sheet.

Roll the pastry around the filling and press the edges together to seal the package, leaving the ends open. Cut the sausage rolls in half, then put them on the lined baking trays, seam-side down, leaving enough room for them to spread. Brush with egg and lightly score the tops diagonally with a sharp knife. Bake for half an hour in a 180°C (350°F/Gas 4) oven until crisp and golden. Serve with lots of tomato or chilli sauce.
Makes 8.

lightly spiced kedgeree

375 g (13 oz) smoked haddock
2 bay leaves
3 slices of lemon
90 g (3¼ oz) butter
1 onion, finely chopped
1/2 tsp mild Indian curry paste
1/2 tsp ground cumin
550 g (3 cups) cooked, cold, long-grain rice
2 tbs chopped parsley
2 tbs lemon juice
125 ml (1/2 cup) whipping cream
3 hard-boiled eggs, peeled and chopped
chopped parsley, extra

Put the haddock, bay leaves and lemon in a frying pan and pour in just enough cold water to cover the cod. Simmer until the fish flakes easily — just under 10 minutes will do. Lift the fish out of the water with a slotted spoon, then drain and cool a little before getting your fork and flaking the flesh into bite-size pieces.

Melt the butter in a large deep frying pan. Once it starts to foam, add the onion, curry paste and cumin and stir for a few minutes — it should be deliciously fragrant. Toss in the rice, fish, parsley and lemon juice and cook until heated through, tossing regularly with two wooden spoons. Add the cream and half the chopped egg and make sure they're mixed in. Garnish with the remaining egg and the extra parsley. Serve with toast. Serves 4.

Formerly a mainstay of the Victorian breakfast table, kedgeree also makes a tasty supper and is considered by many to be more palatable later in the day.

For pure unadulterated soul nourishment, this is one of those comfort foods you just can't go past.

macaroni cheese

225 g (8 oz) macaroni
85 g (3 oz) butter
1 onion, finely chopped
3 tbs plain (all-purpose) flour
500 ml (2 cups) milk
2 tsp wholegrain mustard
155 g (1¼ cups) grated vintage
Cheddar cheese
90 g (¾ cup) grated Cheddar cheese
4 tbs fresh breadcrumbs

Cook the pasta in a pan of boiling salted water until *al dente*. Drain.

While the pasta is cooking, gently cook the onion in a pan of fizzing butter until soft — say 5 minutes. Stir in the flour and cook it briefly until it starts to foam. Take the pan off the heat and gradually pour in the milk, stirring all the time. Put the pan back on the hob and stir constantly until the sauce boils and thickens. Once that happens, lower the heat and simmer for another couple of minutes, then stir in the mustard, most of the cheeses and some salt and pepper. Tumble in the macaroni and toss until the pasta has a gooey, cheesy coating. Tip the whole lot into a greased 1.5 litre (6 cup) ovenproof dish and level the surface.

Make a mixture out of the breadcrumbs and remaining cheese and scatter over the top. Bake in a 180°C (350°F/Gas 4) oven until golden brown and bubbling. The macaroni cheese should be ready to scoff in 15 minutes. Serves 4.

cheese soufflé

melted butter and grated Parmesan,
to coat the soufflé dish
60 g (2¼ oz) butter
4 tbs plain (all-purpose) flour
315 ml (1¼ cups) milk, warmed
185 g (1½ cups) grated Cheddar cheese
1 tsp Dijon mustard
4 eggs, separated
1 tbs grated Parmesan cheese

Lightly grease a 1.5 litre (6 cup) soufflé dish, then roll grated Parmesan around the base and side. Melt the butter in a large saucepan and stir in the flour. Cook for a couple of minutes until it turns a deep ivory colour. Take the pan off the heat, then pour in the milk slowly, whisking until you have a smooth sauce. Return to the heat and bring to the boil. Once this happens, reduce the heat and simmer for a minute before taking off the hob. Add the Cheddar, mustard and egg yolks, and stir until the cheese has melted. Season. Cover the surface with plastic wrap and cool a little.

Whisk the egg whites in a clean dry bowl until stiff peaks form. Using a metal spoon, fold a third of the egg whites into the sauce, then gently but thoroughly fold in the rest — the aim is to maintain volume. Gently scoop the mixture into the soufflé dish. A trick of the trade is to run your thumb or a knife around the edge of the dish to push the mixture slightly away from the edge — this will help it to rise.

Sprinkle with Parmesan and bake for about 25 minutes in a 200°C (400°F/Gas 6) oven until risen and fluffy and light in the middle. Soufflé won't wait for anyone — serve it straight away. Serves 4.

A good soufflé never fails to impress even the most jaded diner. It's something to do with the satisfaction of sinking your spoon into that high-rise of golden perfection.

A timeless dish that's always a hit. Lovely eaten outside on a summer's day and served with a fresh garden salad.

quiche lorraine

155 g (1¼ cups) plain (all-purpose) flour
90 g (3¼ oz) butter, diced and chilled
3 tbs iced water
4 streaky bacon rashers, cut into
short, thin strips
70 g (2½ oz) Gruyère cheese, finely grated
3 eggs
125 ml (½ cup) whipping cream
125 ml (½ cup) milk

Start with the pastry: process the flour and butter in a food processor in short bursts, using the pulse button until it is fine and crumbly. Add most of the water and again process until the mixture just comes together. Turn out onto a lightly floured surface and press into a fat disc. Wrap in plastic wrap and refrigerate for 15 minutes. Now roll the dough out until it's big enough to line a 23 cm (9 inch) fluted flan tin and then lift it into the flan tin and press it in place. Roll the rolling pin over the top of the tin to cut off the excess pastry. Now refrigerate for 15 minutes.

Line the pastry shell with baking paper. Pour in baking beads and bake in a 200°C (400°F/Gas 6) oven for 15 minutes. Remove the paper and beads and return to the oven until the base is dry, about 10 minutes. Let it cool. Lower the temperature to 180°C (350°F/Gas 4). Once the pastry is cool, put it on a baking tray.

Fry the bacon until brown and crisp. Drain, then spread it evenly over the pastry base. Sprinkle the cheese over the bacon. In a jug, whisk together the eggs, cream and milk, then pour it into the pastry shell. Bake for 35–40 minutes, or until set and lightly golden. Serves 6.

party nachos

For the salsa:
3 tomatoes, diced
1 small red onion, finely chopped
3 tbs chopped coriander (cilantro) leaves
1 tbs lime juice
1 garlic clove, crushed
1 small red chilli, seeded and finely chopped
1 avocado

400 g (14 oz) can red kidney beans, rinsed and drained
200 g (7 oz) taco sauce
225 g (8 oz) corn chips
250 g (2 cups) grated Cheddar cheese
sour cream

Start by making the salsa: combine the tomato, onion, coriander, lime juice, garlic and chilli, then cover and set aside.

Heat the kidney beans and taco sauce in a small pan until the sauce boils and the beans are heated through. Spoon a dollop into the middle of four ovenproof plates. Arrange the corn chips around the beans. Sprinkle the beans with cheese, and bake in a 180°C (350°F/Gas 4) oven for 5 minutes, or until the cheese has melted. Meanwhile, peel and dice the avocado, and fold gently through the tomato salsa.

Spoon the salsa on top of the nachos, and serve with a huge dollop of sour cream. Serves 4.

If you prefer hearty beef nachos, heat 1 tablespoon oil in a large heavy-based pan, add 400 g (14 oz) minced (ground) lean beef and cook over medium heat until browned and cooked through. Stir the beef through with the kidney beans and taco sauce until the beef is heated through. Serve as above.

A sociable, communal snack that's great when friends drop around for a drink. Don't forget to pass around the napkins before everyone digs in.

There's something particularly nice about serving your food in an edible dish, whether it's ice cream in a cone or small vegetables within a large one, like these stuffed capsicums.

stuffed capsicums with tomato sauce

4 large red capsicums (peppers)
1 tbs oil
1 leek, thinly sliced
2 garlic cloves, crushed
400 g (14 oz) minced (ground) beef
250 ml (1 cup) chicken or beef stock
3 tbs brown or green lentils
1 potato, peeled and cut into small cubes
2 x 425 g (15 oz) cans chopped tomatoes
2 tbs tomato paste (purée)
3 tbs chopped parsley
3 tbs chopped basil
3 tbs red wine
1/2 tsp caster (superfine) sugar
1 bay leaf
40 g (1/2 cup) fresh breadcrumbs
25 g (1 oz) butter, melted
2 tsp finely chopped parsley, extra

Slice off the stalk end of the capsicums and remove the seeds and membranes. Cut a sliver off the bottom of each capsicum so that they can sit flat without wobbling.

Soften the leek and garlic in the hot oil in a frying pan. Add the beef and cook until nicely browned. Next, add the stock, lentils, potato, one of the cans of tomatoes and half the tomato paste. Bring to the boil, then reduce the heat and simmer for 30 minutes until the potato and lentils are tender and the mixture is thick. Stir in the herbs and salt and pepper.

Spoon the mixture into the capsicums, then sit them in a shallow ovenproof dish. Heat the remaining can of tomatoes and tomato paste and the wine, sugar and bay leaf in a small pan, season and then pour around the capsicums.

Make a crumble out of the breadcrumbs, butter and parsley, then sprinkle this over the capsicums. If you want the whole stuffed capsicum experience, you can cook the lids too. Pop the whole lot in a 180°C (350°F/Gas 4) oven for 30 minutes. If you're doing the lids, top the capsicums with their lids, then serve. Serves 4.

coulibiac

60 g (2¼ oz) butter
1 onion, finely chopped
200 g (7 oz) button mushrooms, sliced
2 tbs lemon juice
225 g (8 oz) salmon fillet, boned, skinned, cut into 2 cm (¾ inch) pieces
2 hard-boiled eggs, chopped
2 tbs dill, chopped
2 tbs parsley, chopped
185 g (1 cup) cooked long-grain rice
3 tbs cream
375 g (13 oz) packet frozen puff pastry
1 egg, lightly beaten, for glazing

Melt half the butter in a frying pan and when it's sizzling, cook the onion slowly until soft but not browned. Add the mushrooms and cook for 5 minutes before stirring in the lemon juice. Spoon the whole mixture into a bowl.

Melt the rest of the butter in the pan and when it's fizzing, add the salmon and cook for 2 minutes. Remove the pan from the heat, cool slightly and add the egg, dill, parsley and salt and pepper. Mix gently and set aside. Combine the rice and cream in a small bowl.

Divide the pastry in two and roll out one piece to an 18 x 30 cm (7 x 12 inch) rectangle and the other slightly larger. Lay the smaller one on a lightly greased baking tray. The idea with this pie is to create layers in the centre, leaving a 3 cm (1¼ inch) border. The first layer uses half the rice, the next the salmon, then the mushroom and, to finish, the rest of the rice.

Lay the pastry over the filling. Seal the edges then crimp. Cool for half an hour, then brush with beaten egg. Bake in a preheated 210°C (415°F/Gas 6–7) oven. After 15 minutes, reduce the heat to 180°C (350°F/Gas 4) and bake until golden, about 15 minutes. Serves 4–6.

You can substitute chicken for the fish in this traditional Russian pie, or go for something slightly more exotic, like eel.

Any type of pasta can be used for minestrone, though smaller shapes are easier to manage on a soup spoon. The Milanese version uses rice.

hearty minestrone

1 tbs olive oil
1 onion, finely chopped
2 garlic cloves, crushed
2 carrots, diced
2 potatoes, peeled and diced
2 celery stalks, finely chopped
2 zucchini (courgettes), finely chopped
125 g (4 1/2 oz) green beans, chopped
150 g (2 cups) shredded cabbage
2 litres (8 cups) beef stock
425 g (15 oz) can chopped tomatoes
80 g (1/2 cup) macaroni
450 g (1 lb) can borlotti or red
kidney beans, drained
grated Parmesan cheese
sprigs of thyme

Warm the oil in a large, heavy-based pan, then slowly cook the onion and garlic until the onion is softened but not browned — 5 minutes will do. Add the carrot, potato and celery and cook for another 5 minutes, stirring a few times.

Now do the same with the zucchini, green beans and cabbage. Add the stock and chopped tomatoes. Bring slowly to the boil, then reduce the heat, cover and leave to simmer away for 2 hours.

Toss in the macaroni and beans and cook until the pasta is tender — 15 minutes should be enough. Ladle the hot soup into generous bowls, sprinkle with Parmesan and garnish with a sprig of thyme.
Serves 8.

welsh rarebit

125 g (4½ oz) Cheddar cheese
30 g (1 oz) unsalted butter, softened
2 tsp English mustard
1 egg, beaten
1 tbs beer (Guinness or stout)
1 tsp Worcestershire sauce
6 slices of bread

Grate the cheese on the fine side of the cheese grater, then make a cheesy mash of it and the butter, mustard, egg, beer, Worcestershire sauce and salt and freshly ground black pepper.

Toast the bread on both sides and then spread the top of each piece with a generous amount of the cheesy mixture. Grill under a hot grill until browned, bubbling and meltingly irresistible.
Serves 4.

Also known as Welsh rabbit, this cheesy snack has a number of variations. English rabbit uses red wine rather than beer, American rabbit uses whisked egg whites rather than whole eggs, and Yorkshire rabbit is topped with bacon and a poached egg.

sweet satisfaction

It takes only three ingredients to create one of the creamiest, most delicious desserts ever tasted. It's best if refrigerated overnight, but it could prove difficult to wait that long.

creamy chocolate mousse

125 g (4½ oz) good-quality dark
chocolate, chopped
4 eggs, separated
185 ml (¾ cup) cream, lightly whipped

Melt the chocolate in a bowl balanced over a saucepan of gently simmering water (without letting the bowl touch the water). Stir the chocolate occasionally until it's melted, then take it off the heat to cool slightly. Lightly beat the egg yolks and stir them into the melted chocolate, then gently fold in the cream until velvety.

Beat the egg whites to soft peaks. Fold one spoonful of the fluffy egg white into the mousse with a metal spoon, then gently fold in the remainder — the secret is to use a light, quick touch.

You only need small quantities of the mousse — you can either serve it in six small wine glasses or 185 ml (¾ cup) ramekins. Cover with plastic wrap and refrigerate for 4 hours or overnight till set. When you're ready to serve, you can either add a jaunty curl of whipped cream or a dusting of cocoa powder. Serves 6.

crêpes suzette

For the crepes:
250 g (9 oz) plain (all-purpose) flour
1 tsp sugar
2 eggs, lightly beaten
400 ml (14 fl oz) milk
1 tbs melted butter
2 tbs grated orange zest
1 tbs grated lemon zest
butter or oil, for frying

125 g ($\frac{1}{2}$ cup) caster (superfine) sugar
250 ml (1 cup) orange juice
1 tbs grated orange zest
2 tbs brandy or Cognac
2 tbs Grand Marnier
50 g ($1\frac{3}{4}$ oz) unsalted butter, diced

To make the crepes, sift the flour into a bowl and make a mound out of it. Add the sugar and a pinch of salt, then make a dip in the top. Mix the eggs, milk and 100 ml ($3\frac{1}{2}$ fl oz) water together and then pour slowly into the hole, whisking all the time to incorporate the flour until you have a smooth, creamy batter. Stir in the melted butter, then rest for 20 minutes.

Stir the citrus zest into the batter. Heat and grease a well-seasoned frying pan. Pour in enough batter to coat the base of the pan in a thin layer. Cook over moderate heat for a minute until the crepe starts to come away from the side of the pan then turn and cook the other side until light gold. Repeat with the remaining batter. Fold the crepes in four.

Melt the sugar in a large frying pan over low heat and cook to a rich caramel, tilting the pan so it browns evenly. Pour in the orange juice and zest and boil for 2 minutes. Put the crepes in the pan and spoon the sauce over them. Add the brandy and Grand Marnier and flambé by lighting with a match (stand back and keep a pan lid handy). Add the butter and shake the pan until it melts. Serve immediately. Serves 6.

Part of the fun of ordering crêpes Suzette at a restaurant is watching the waiter flambé it at the table for you. It may be a little hard to do in your own dining room, but if you're game, then give it a go.

This looks just as good as you'd buy at the bakery, and tastes even better because you made it yourself. Serve it with a refreshing glass of homemade lemonade.

fruit flan

For the shortcrust pastry:
185 g (1½ cups) plain (all-purpose) flour
2 tbs caster (superfine) sugar
125 g (4½ oz) unsalted butter, diced and chilled
2–3 tbs iced water

For the filling:
3 egg yolks
3 tbs caster (superfine) sugar
2 tbs plain (all-purpose) flour
250 ml (1 cup) milk
1 tsp natural vanilla extract
strawberries, halved
kiwi fruit, peeled and sliced
blueberries
apricot jam

Process the flour, sugar and butter together in a food processor using the pulse button in short bursts until fine and crumbly. Add the water and again process until it just comes together. Turn out onto a lightly floured surface and press into a ball, then roll out to fit a 23 cm (9 inch) flan tin. Line the tin with pastry and trim off the excess, then refrigerate for 20 minutes. Prick the bottom of the pastry shell, then line it with crumpled baking paper and fill with baking beads. Bake for 15 minutes in a 190°C (375°F/Gas 5) oven, then remove the paper and beads and bake for another 20 minutes, until cooked. Cool completely.

For the filling, whisk the egg yolks in a bowl with the sugar until light and creamy, then whisk in the flour. Bring the milk to the boil, then pour slowly into the egg mixture, whisking constantly. Pour into a pan and bring to the boil over medium heat, whisking until large bubbles break on the surface. Transfer to a bowl, stir in the vanilla, and cool to room temperature, stirring frequently. Cover the surface with plastic wrap and refrigerate until cold. Spoon the custard into the pastry shell, then arrange the fruit. Heat the jam until liquid, then strain. Glaze the fruit with the jam. Serves 6.

black forest gateau

200 g (7 oz) unsalted butter
185 g (3/4 cup) caster sugar
3 eggs, lightly beaten
1 tsp natural vanilla extract
210 g (1 2/3 cups) self-raising flour
40 g (1/3 cup) plain (all-purpose) flour
90 g (3/4 cup) cocoa powder
1 tbs instant coffee granules
125 ml (1/2 cup) buttermilk
4 tbs milk
315 ml (1 1/4 cups) cream, whipped
425 g (14 oz) can pitted cherries, drained
chocolate curls
cherries with stems

For the chocolate icing:
300 g (10 1/2 oz) dark chocolate, chopped
375 g (13 oz) unsalted butter, chopped

Beat the butter and sugar together until creamy. Add the eggs bit by bit along with the vanilla, beating the mixture well — if it starts to split at this point don't worry, it will come back together later. Sift the flours and cocoa into the bowl and add the coffee and 1/4 teaspoon salt, then add the buttermilk and milk. Fold the mixture together with a large spoon and spoon it into a lined 23 cm (9 inch) round springform cake tin. Bake in a 180°C (350°F/Gas 4) oven for 1–1 1/4 hours, or until a skewer comes out clean. Cool for 30 minutes, then turn out.

To make the icing, melt the chocolate until it is smooth and liquid and then cool it for 30 minutes to thicken it again. Beat the butter until creamy, then add the melted chocolate, beating until you have a smooth spreadable mixture.

Cut the cake into three layers. Divide the whipped cream and cherries between the two middle layers and sandwich the cake together. Spread most of the icing over the top and side of the cake, then using your decorating talents pipe the remaining icing around the top and finish with chocolate curls and cherries. Serves 8–10.

This baroque confection, a frivolous mixture of cream, chocolate and cherries, had its moment of worldwide domination in the late twentieth century as the jewel of the dessert menu.

This citrus tart gets its name from Key West – a seaport in Florida. Definitely a dessert to welcome home the sailors.

key lime pie

125 g (4 1/2 oz) sweet wheatmeal biscuits
85 g (3 oz) unsalted butter, melted
4 egg yolks
400 g (14 oz) can condensed milk
125 ml (1/2 cup) lime juice
2 tsp finely grated lime zest
250 ml (1 cup) cream, whipped
lime zest, for garnish

Blitz the biscuits in a food processor for 30 seconds until finely crushed. Tumble into a bowl and stir in the butter until the crumbs are well moistened. Press the mixture into a 23 cm (9 inch) pie dish and cool in the fridge until it feels firm.

Beat the yolks, condensed milk, lime juice and zest in a large bowl until thick and luscious — electric beaters are great for this. Pour into the crust and smooth the surface. Bake for 20–25 minutes in a 180°C (350°F/Gas 4) oven until set.

Allow the pie to cool a little before chilling it completely in the fridge — you'll probably need to leave 2 hours for this. Let your inner artist have its way and go wild decorating the pie with whipped cream and spirals of lime zest.
Serves 8.

sticky date pudding

185 g (1 cup) chopped pitted dates
1 tsp bicarbonate of soda
90 g (3¼ oz) unsalted butter, softened
115 g (½ cup) firmly packed soft brown sugar
2 eggs, lightly beaten
1 tsp natural vanilla extract
185 g (1½ cups) self-raising flour

For the sauce:
230 g (1 cup) firmly packed soft brown sugar
250 ml (1 cup) whipping cream
90 g (3¼ oz) unsalted butter
½ tsp natural vanilla extract

Put the dates and soda in a heatproof bowl and add 250 ml (1 cup) boiling water. Stir and leave for 15 minutes.

Beat the butter and brown sugar until light and creamy, then gradually beat in the eggs and then the vanilla. Fold in half of the sifted flour then half of the date mixture. Stir in the remaining flour and dates, mixing well. Pour into a lined, deep 18 cm (7 inch) square cake tin and bake for 50 minutes in a 180°C (350°F/Gas 4) oven until cooked when tested with a skewer. Leave the pudding in the tin to cool for 10 minutes, then turn out.

While the pudding is cooling, make the sauce. Put the sugar, cream, butter and vanilla in a pan and bring to the boil while stirring. Reduce the heat and simmer for 5 minutes until you have a gloriously fudgy, sticky sauce. Serve portions of the pudding with the sauce. Serves 8.

You might know this scrumptious dessert by its other name, Sticky toffee pudding.

If it wasn't called a pudding, this is the sort of dessert you'd eat all year round, not just over winter. If you can't wait for the cold spell to arrive before making it, just pour the sauce over the top of the cake, refrigerate, and serve with a scoop of ice cream.

The beauty of banana fritters is that they are made from ingredients you're likely to already have in the house, and don't require too much preparation — exactly what you need when sweet cravings strike unexpectedly.

banana fritters

125 g (1 cup) self-raising flour
1 tbs caster (superfine) sugar
1 tsp ground cinnamon
4 bananas
oil, for deep-frying

Sift the flour and a pinch of salt into a bowl. Make a well in the centre, and gradually add 250 ml (1 cup) water while gently whisking, drawing the flour in from the sides. Whisk until just combined. Don't worry if the batter looks a bit lumpy — it should. Stand for 30 minutes. Combine the sugar and cinnamon in a bowl, and set aside.

Cut the bananas in half crossways, slightly on the diagonal. Dip them into the batter. Quickly drain off any excess batter and deep-fry for 2 minutes, or until crisp and golden. The best way to do this is to use two pairs of tongs — one to dip the bananas in the batter and lift into the oil, and one to remove from the oil. You could also use a slotted spoon to lift the cooked fritters. Drain on paper towels. Repeat with the remaining bananas. Sprinkle with the cinnamon sugar and serve with ice cream or cream.
Serves 4.

baked alaska

2 litres (8 cups) good-quality vanilla ice cream
250 g (9 oz) mixed glacé fruit, finely chopped
125 ml (1/2 cup) Grand Marnier or Cointreau
2 tsp grated orange zest
60 g (21/4 oz) toasted almonds, finely chopped
60 g (21/4 oz) dark chocolate, finely chopped
1 sponge or butter cake, cut into 3 cm (11/4 inch) slices
3 egg whites
185 g (3/4 cup) caster (superfine) sugar

Line a 2 litre (8 cup) pudding basin with damp muslin. Soften half of the ice cream enough that you can fold in the glacé fruit with a couple of tablespoons of the liqueur and 1 teaspoon of the orange zest. Spoon into the basin, smooth over the base and up the sides, then freeze until hard. Soften the remaining ice cream and fold in the almonds, chocolate, remaining liqueur and orange zest. Spoon into the frozen shell and smooth the surface. Work quickly to evenly cover the ice cream with one layer of cake. Cover with foil and freeze for 2 hours.

Beat the egg whites into soft peaks. Gradually add the sugar, beating well after each addition. Beat for 4–5 minutes, until thick and glossy. Unmould the ice cream onto an ovenproof dish and remove the muslin. Quickly spread the meringue over the top to cover the ice cream completely. Bake for 5–8 minutes in a 220°C (425°F/Gas 7) oven until lightly browned. Cut into wedges and serve at once. Serves 6–8.

If you're feeling flamboyant, partly bury an upturned half egg shell in the top of the meringue before baking. Fill with warmed brandy and set alight to serve.

The culinary equivalent of rolling around in the snow before jumping into a hot spa or sauna. Cold in the centre with an insulating layer on the outside, each spoonful will send your temperature soaring.

A little bit of this and a touch of that … trifle is composed of any number of delectable bits and pieces. Go with a simple version, or add jelly, fruit, crushed meringues or anything else that takes your fancy.

trifle

4 slices of Madeira (pound) cake
or trifle sponges
3 tbs sweet sherry or Madeira
250 g (1 punnet) raspberries
4 eggs
2 tbs caster (superfine) sugar
2 tbs plain (all-purpose) flour
500 ml (2 cups) milk
1/4 tsp natural vanilla extract
125 ml (1/2 cup) cream, whipped
3 tbs flaked almonds
raspberries

Pull out your fanciest bowl and put the cake in the base of it, then sprinkle it with the sherry. Scatter the raspberries over the top and crush them gently into the sponge with the back of a spoon to release their tart flavour, leaving some of them whole.

Mix the eggs, sugar and flour together in a bowl. Heat the milk in a pan, pour it over the egg mixture, stir well and pour back into a clean pan. Cook over medium heat until the custard boils and thickens and coats the back of a spoon. Stir in the vanilla, cover the surface with plastic wrap and leave to cool.

Pour the cooled custard over the raspberries and leave to set in the fridge — it will firm up but not become solid. Spoon the whipped cream over the custard. Go wild decorating with almonds and raspberries (or anything else you fancy) and refrigerate until needed. Serves 6.

hot chocolate soufflé

25 g (1 oz) butter, melted
caster sugar, to sprinkle
175 g (6 oz) good-quality dark
chocolate, chopped
5 egg yolks, lightly beaten
3 tbs caster (superfine) sugar
7 egg whites
icing (confectioners') sugar, to dust

Wrap a double layer of baking paper around six 250 ml (1 cup) ramekins, to come 3 cm (1¼ inches) above the rim. Secure with string. Brush the insides with melted butter, sprinkle with caster sugar, shake to coat evenly, then tip out the excess. Place on a baking tray.

Melt the chocolate in a bowl balanced over a saucepan of gently simmering water (without letting the bowl touch the water). Stir the chocolate occasionally until it's melted, then take it off the heat to cool slightly. Stir in the egg yolks and sugar. Dollop the chocolate goo into a large bowl. Beat the egg whites into firm peaks.

Take a clean spoon and add a big dollop of the whisked whites to the chocolate goo to loosen it. Lightly fold in the rest of the egg white until just combined. Divide the mixture among the ramekins and bake in a 200°C (400°F/Gas 6) oven for 12–15 minutes, or until well risen and just set. Cut the string and remove the collars. Serve immediately, dusted lightly with the sifted icing sugar.
Serves 6.

There are few things as decadent as serving up individual soufflés at home, and the result is well worth the effort. Expect a round of applause when they appear.

Originating in Treviso, Italy, this rich dessert has appeared in many guises over the years. That shot of caffeine still acts as a 'pick me up', the literal translation of its name.

tiramisu

375 ml (1¹/2 cups) espresso coffee
500 g (1 lb 2 oz) mascarpone
2 tbs caster (superfine) sugar
185 ml (³/4 cup) Kahlúa or Tia Maria
125 ml (¹/2 cup) cream, lightly whipped
250 g (9 oz) thin sponge finger biscuits
4 tbs cocoa powder

Pour the coffee into a shallow dish. Mix the mascarpone, sugar and liqueur in a large bowl until you have a thick mass, then gently fold in the cream. Cover with some plastic wrap then put in the fridge. Dip half the sponge finger biscuits into the coffee (move quickly so that they don't go soggy), and lay them out in a single layer on the bottom of a 2 litre (8 cup) ceramic dish. Spread half of the mascarpone mixture over the biscuits and dust liberally with half of the cocoa (it's easy if you use a fine sieve).

Dunk the rest of the biscuits in the coffee and add a layer of them before spreading with the remaining mascarpone mixture. Dust with the remaining cocoa, then cover and keep in the fridge overnight to allow the flavours to develop before serving.
Serves 8.

crème brûlée

500 ml (2 cups) whipping cream
200 ml (7 fl oz) milk
125 g (1/2 cup) caster (superfine) sugar
1 vanilla bean
5 egg yolks
1 egg white
1 tbs orange flower water
100 g (3 1/2 oz) demerara sugar

Put the cream, milk and half the sugar in a saucepan with the vanilla bean. Bring just to the boil so that the delicate flavour of the vanilla infuses into the liquid.

Meanwhile, mix together the remaining sugar with the egg yolks and white. Strain the boiling milk over the egg mixture, whisking well, then stir in the orange flower water.

Ladle into eight 125 ml (1/2 cup) ramekins, then sit the ramekins in a roasting tin. Pour enough hot water into the tin to come halfway up the sides of the ramekins. Bake in a 120°C (250°F/Gas 1/2) oven for 1 1/2 hours, or until set in the centre. Cool and refrigerate until ready to serve. Just before serving, sprinkle the tops with demerara sugar and caramelize under a very hot grill or with a blowtorch (the small chef's variety, not the welder's!). Serve immediately.
Serves 8.

The crisp topping is a delicious contrast to the creamy custard beneath. Add a little drama to the night by using a blowtorch to caramelize the sugar.

A lovely gooey centre under a sticky, gooey meringue. Little wonder that children grow up to cook it for their own kids.

lemon meringue pie

For the pastry:
375 g (13 oz) bought sweet shortcrust pastry
or home-made pastry from page 201

For the filling and topping:
3 tbs cornflour (cornstarch)
3 tbs plain (all-purpose) flour
250 g (1 cup) caster (superfine) sugar
185 ml (3/4 cup) lemon juice
3 tsp grated lemon zest
40 g (1 1/2 oz) unsalted butter
6 eggs, separated
375 g (1 1/2 cups) caster (superfine)
sugar, extra
pinch of cream of tartar

Roll the dough out until it is large enough to line a greased 23 cm (9 inch) round pie plate, then ease it into the prepared dish. Trim away the excess pastry and crimp the edge with a fork. Leave in the fridge for 15 minutes. Now line the pastry with a sheet of crumpled baking paper and fill with baking beads. Bake in a 180°C (350°F/Gas 4) oven for 12 minutes, then remove the paper and beads, and bake for a further 10 minutes until the pastry is cooked. Remove from the oven and leave to cool.

To make the filling, place the flours and sugar in a pan. Whisk in the lemon juice, zest and 375 ml (1 1/2 cups) water. Whisk continually over medium heat until the mixture boils and thickens, then reduce the heat and cook for 1 minute. Remove from the heat, then whisk in the butter and egg yolks, one at a time.

Spread the filling into the pastry shell. Beat the egg whites and extra sugar for 10 minutes until thick and glossy. Beat in the cream of tartar. Spread the meringue over the top of the pie, piling it high towards the centre and making peaks with a knife. Bake in a 220°C (425°F/Gas 7) oven for 5–10 minutes until lightly browned.
Serves 6.

bread and butter pudding

80 g (1/2 cup) mixed raisins and sultanas
2 tbs brandy or rum
30 g (1 oz) unsalted butter
4 slices good-quality white bread
or brioche loaf
3 eggs
3 tbs caster (superfine) sugar
750 ml (3 cups) milk
3 tbs cream
1/4 tsp natural vanilla extract
1/4 tsp ground cinnamon
1 tbs demerara sugar

Soak the raisins and sultanas in the liquor until they become plump, drunken treasures — half an hour should be long enough. Butter the slices of bread or brioche and cut each piece into eight triangles. Arrange the bread in a 1 litre (4 cup) ovenproof dish.

Mix the eggs with the sugar, add the milk, cream, vanilla and cinnamon and mix well. Drain the raisins and sultanas and add any liquid to the custard.

Scatter the soaked raisins and sultanas over the bread and pour the custard over the top. Cover with plastic wrap and refrigerate for 1 hour to let the flavours intensify.

Remove the pudding from the fridge and sprinkle with the demerara sugar. Bake for 35–40 minutes in a 180°C (350°F/Gas 4) oven until the custard is set and the top crunchy and golden.
Serves 4.

Use good-quality bread for this recipe. Ordinary sliced white bread will tend to go a bit claggy when it soaks up the milk.

You can reinvent this old favourite by using slices of fruit loaf instead of plain bread, or opting for rich chocolate-flavoured brioche or croissants.

Further proof, as if you needed it, that what goes around, comes around. The ideal party dessert for flower children of the new millennium.

chocolate fondue

250 g (9 oz) good-quality dark chocolate, chopped
125 ml (1/2 cup) thick (double/heavy) cream
fresh fruit

Place the chocolate and cream in a fondue pot and melt it gently, stirring occasionally until you have a thick, rich chocolately goo. Fire up the fondue burner, sit the pot on top and start dunking the fresh fruit with forks or skewers.
Serves 6–8.

If you've still got a melon baller hidden in your kitchen drawer, now's the time to dig it out to scoop out gorgeous balls of fruit and think of it as all part of the fondue experience. Fruits that work well in fondues include strawberries, pears, cherries and bananas.

tea time

To savour the full Viennese experience, serve the Sachertorte with a pot of your very best coffee and Mozart playing softly in the background.

sachertorte

125 g (1 cup) plain (all-purpose) flour
3 tbs cocoa powder
250 g (1 cup) caster (superfine) sugar
100 g (3½ oz) unsalted butter
3 tbs strawberry jam
4 eggs, separated

For the ganache topping:
170 ml (²/₃ cup) whipping cream
4 tbs caster (superfine) sugar
200 g (7 oz) dark chocolate, chopped

Make a mound of sifted flour and cocoa in a large bowl, then make a little dent in the top. Slowly heat the sugar, butter and half the jam in a small saucepan until the butter melts and the sugar dissolves, then pour it over the flour, then add the lightly beaten egg yolks. Now stir briefly until just combined.

Beat the egg whites in a small bowl until you have a cloud of soft peaks. Stir a big dollop of the egg white into the cake mixture, then fold in the rest in two batches. Pour into a lined 20 cm (8 inch) round cake tin and smooth the surface. Bake in a 180°C (350°F/Gas 4) oven for about 45 minutes. When cooked, rest for 15 minutes, then turn out onto a wire rack.

To make the topping, stir the cream, sugar and chocolate together in a small saucepan over low heat until you have a smooth liquid.

Trim the top of the cake flat, then turn it upside down on a wire rack over a tray. Melt the remaining jam and brush it over the cake. Pour most of the topping over the cake and tap the tray to flatten the surface. Place the remaining mixture in a piping bag and pipe 'Sacher' on the top of the cake.
Serves 10.

pineapple upside-down cake

90 g (3¼ oz) unsalted butter, melted
95 g (½ cup) soft brown sugar
450 g (1 lb) can pineapple rings
in natural juice
6 glacé cherries
125 g (4½ oz) unsalted butter, extra, diced
185 g (¾ cup) caster (superfine) sugar
2 eggs
1 tsp natural vanilla extract
185 g (1½ cups) self-raising flour
60 g (½ cup) plain (all-purpose) flour
4 tbs desiccated coconut

Pour the melted butter into a 20 cm (8 inch) round tin, brushing some of it up the side, but leaving most on the base. Sprinkle the brown sugar over the base, where it will melt into a sticky goo. Drain the pineapple, but keep 125 ml (½ cup) of the juice. Arrange the pineapple rings over the base of the tin and dot a cheery cherry in the centre of each ring.

Beat the butter and the sugar together until fluffy, then add the eggs one at a time, beating well after each one. Stir in the vanilla and beat until combined. Sift the flours into the butter mixture, then add the coconut and reserved pineapple juice. Fold in with a metal spoon until just combined. Spoon the mixture evenly into the tin over the pineapple rings and smooth the surface. Indent the centre slightly with the back of a spoon — this will ensure the cake has a reasonably flat base.

Bake in a 180°C (350°F/Gas 4) oven for about an hour until cooked. An easy way to check this is to insert a skewer into the cake, and if it comes out clean, it's done. Leave the cake in the tin for 10 minutes before turning it out onto a plate.
Serves 6.

Looks good, tastes good and with all those yummy fruity bits, it must be good for you ... well, two out of three ain't bad.

Beautiful served in the warmer months with fresh strawberries or a variety of seasonal berries. Have two helpings if you feel you need to up your calcium intake.

baked cheesecake

375 g (13 oz) plain sweet biscuits
175 g (6 oz) unsalted butter, melted

For the filling:
500 g (1 lb 2 oz) cream cheese
200 g (7 oz) caster (superfine) sugar
4 eggs
300 ml (10$\frac{1}{2}$ fl oz) whipping cream
2 tbs plain (all-purpose) flour
1 tsp ground cinnamon
$\frac{1}{4}$ tsp freshly grated nutmeg
1 tbs lemon juice
2 tsp natural vanilla extract
freshly grated nutmeg
ground cinnamon

Blitz the biscuits in a food processor until they are crushed into fine crumbs. Add the melted butter and whiz for another 10 seconds. Press the mixture into the base and side of a lightly greased 23 cm (9 inch) shallow springform tin, then pop it in the fridge for an hour.

Beat the cream cheese and sugar together, then add the eggs and cream and beat for about 4 minutes. Fold in the flour, cinnamon, nutmeg, juice and vanilla. Pour the mixture into the chilled crust. Bake in a 180°C (350°F/Gas 4) oven for an hour without opening the oven door, until the cheesecake is golden brown on top. Now it's time to cool the cheesecake — a gradual process that should help prevent it from sinking and cracking. Turn off the heat and let the cake stand in the oven for 2 hours. Then open the oven door and let it stand for a further hour. Lastly, refrigerate overnight. For a decorative touch, sprinkle with nutmeg and cinnamon and then serve. Delicious with lashings of cream and some strawberries.
Serves 10.

coconut jam slice

125 g (1 cup) plain (all-purpose) flour
60 g (1/2 cup) self-raising flour
150 g (51/2 oz) unsalted butter
60 g (1/2 cup) icing (confectioners') sugar
1 egg yolk
160 g (1/2 cup) strawberry jam

For the topping:
125 g (1/2 cup) caster (superfine) sugar
3 eggs
270 g (3 cups) desiccated coconut, toasted

Lightly grease a shallow 23 cm (9 inch) square cake tin, then line the base with baking paper, keeping the paper long enough to hang over two opposite sides — this makes it easy to lift the cooked slice out of the tin.

Put the flours, butter and icing sugar in a food processor, then mix in short bursts until the mixture is fine and crumbly. Add the egg yolk and blitz until the mixture just comes together. Press the dough into the prepared tin and then refrigerate for 10 minutes.

Bake in a 180°C (350°F/Gas 4) oven for 15 minutes, or until golden brown. Leave somewhere to cool, then spread jam over the cooled base.

To make the topping, whisk the sugar and eggs together until creamy, then stir in the coconut. Spread the topping over the jam, pressing down with the back of a spoon. Bake for another 20–30 minutes until lightly golden. Leave it to cool completely in the tin, then lift the slice out, using the paper as handles. Cut into pieces and enjoy.
Makes about 20.

This is the slice to make when you need something sweet, fast. It doesn't take long to make, and it probably won't last too long untouched, either.

Wherever you live and whatever time of the year you serve it, just one bite of this scrumptious slice and you too will always dream of a white Christmas.

white christmas

45 g (1¹/₂ cups) puffed rice cereal
100 g (1 cup) milk powder
125 g (1 cup) icing (confectioners') sugar
90 g (1 cup) desiccated coconut
4 tbs chopped red glacé cherries
4 tbs chopped green glacé cherries
4 tbs sultanas
250 g (9 oz) copha (white vegetable shortening)

Combine the cereal, powdered milk, sugar, coconut and fruit in a large mixing bowl. Make a well in the centre.

Melt the shortening over low heat, then let it cool slightly. Scoop it into the dry ingredients, then stir until all the ingredients are moist.

Now spoon the mixture into a foil-lined 28 x 18 cm (11 x 7 inch) tin and smooth the surface. Refrigerate for 30 minutes, by which time it should be set. Cut it into small triangles to serve or take to the bake sale. Makes 24.

bakewell slice

125 g (1 cup) plain (all-purpose) flour
90 g (3¼ oz) unsalted butter, diced
1 tbs caster (superfine) sugar

For the topping:
175 g (6 oz) unsalted butter
185 g (¾ cup) caster (superfine) sugar
3 eggs, lightly beaten
185 g (1 cup) ground almonds
90 g (¾ cup) plain (all-purpose) flour
210 g (⅔ cup) raspberry jam
4 tbs flaked almonds

Lightly grease a shallow 20 x 30 cm (8 x 12 inch) tin. Line the base with baking paper, extending over the two long sides. Put the flour, butter and sugar in a food processor, then use the pulse action and blitz briefly until you've got what looks like fine crumbs. Add a tablespoon of water and blitz again very briefly until the mixture comes together.

Turn the dough into the prepared tin, pressing evenly over the base using lightly floured hands. Bake in a 210°C (415°F/Gas 6–7) oven for 5 minutes, then remove from the oven and allow to cool. Reduce the oven to 180°C (350°F/Gas 4).

To make the topping, beat the butter and sugar in a small bowl until light and creamy. Add the eggs gradually, beating thoroughly after each addition. Transfer to a large bowl, then add the ground almonds and flour. Use a wooden spoon to stir until just combined.

Spread the pastry base with jam. Spread evenly with topping and sprinkle with flaked almonds. Bake for 25–30 minutes or until lightly golden, then leave somewhere to cool in its tin. When it's cold, cut into fingers. Makes 18.

It's so tempting to imagine that the town of Bakewell in Derbyshire is home to some of England's top-notch chefs, that we won't worry too much about reality. The slice named for the town attests that at least someone there can cook.

Ever feel that mid-afternoon slump? A piece of caramel slice will give you a burst of energy to get through the rest of the day.

caramel slice

3 tbs plain (all-purpose) flour
3 tbs self-raising flour
45 g (1/2 cup) desiccated coconut
3 tbs soft brown sugar
50 g (1¾ oz) unsalted butter

For the filling:
60 g (2¼ oz) unsalted butter
4 tbs golden syrup
2 x 400 g (14 oz) cans condensed milk

For the topping:
125 g (4½ oz) dark chocolate, chopped
30 g (1 oz) unsalted butter

First of all, line a shallow 28 x 18 cm (11 x 7 inch) tin with foil — cover the sides as well as the bottom. Sift the flours into a bowl, then stir in the coconut and make a dip in the top. Melt the sugar and butter in a small pan, then pour the buttery caramel into the dry ingredients and give a good stir. Use the back of a spoon to press the mixture into your tin. Now bake in a 180°C (350°F/Gas 4) oven for 10 minutes before cooling in the tin.

Next, make the filling. To do this, combine the butter, golden syrup and condensed milk in a small saucepan. Stir constantly over low heat for about 10 minutes until the mixture boils and lightly browns. Pour over the pastry base and bake for 20 minutes. Cool completely.

Finally, to make the topping, put the chocolate and butter in a heatproof bowl and balance the bowl over a saucepan of simmering water until you have a smooth, glossy mixture. Take the bowl off the heat and let the chocolate cool a bit before spreading over the caramel filling. Let it set, then use the foil to lift the whole thing out of the tin. Cut into squares and start gobbling. Makes 18.

rich chocolate truffles

185 ml (3/4 cup) thick (double/heavy) cream
400 g (14 oz) best-quality dark
chocolate, grated
70 g (2½ oz) unsalted butter, diced
2 tbs Cointreau
dark cocoa powder, for rolling

If you can, start these the day before you want to serve them. Dollop the cream into a small saucepan and bring to the boil. Take the pan off the heat, then stir in the chocolate until it is completely melted, then add the butter and do the same. Stir in the Cointreau, then spoon the chocolate goo into a large bowl, cover and refrigerate for several hours or overnight — the aim is to get the mixture firm enough to be able to roll it.

Once you have a thick, chocolately mass, you can start rolling it into balls, but you'll need to work quickly so that it doesn't melt. You can make the balls as large as you like — a tablespoon of mixture per ball is about a mouthful. Put the balls on a lined baking tray and chill them until firm. Once they are hard, roll them in cocoa, shake off any excess and return to the fridge. About half an hour before you want to serve them, take them out of the fridge so they're at room temperature. Makes about 30.

Every meal, no matter how good, can be improved with a little chocolate. You don't have to serve a lot, just a taste will ensure your evening finishes on the perfect note.

These are impossible to eat quietly, so enjoy the crunch as you bite through the crisp biscuit and hit the creamy centre. Lovely served with coffee and a nip of brandy.

brandy snaps

60 g (2¼ oz) unsalted butter
2 tbs golden syrup
4 tbs soft brown sugar
3 tbs plain (all-purpose) flour
1½ tsp ground ginger

For the coffee liqueur cream:
170 ml (⅔ cup) whipping cream
1 tbs icing (confectioners') sugar, sifted
1 tsp instant coffee powder
1 tbs coffee liqueur

Melt the butter, syrup and sugar in a small saucepan, stirring often. Take the pan off the heat, then stir in the sifted flour and ginger with a wooden spoon — use a light touch.

There are a couple of tricks to brandy snaps — prepare only a few at a time and leave plenty of room between each one. Dollop some mixture (a level teaspoon is good) onto a lined baking tray. Keep going until you've got four altogether. Use a palette knife to spread each dollop into an 8 cm (3 inch) round. Bake in a 180°C (350°F/Gas 4) oven for 6 minutes until lightly browned. Leave them alone for 30 seconds, then lift off and wrap around the handle of a wooden spoon while still hot. If the biscuits harden, pop them in the oven again to soften, then roll. Once you have nice neat rolls, let them cool while you do the same with the rest of the mixture.

To make the filling, combine all the ingredients in a small bowl and stir until just combined. Cover and refrigerate for an hour, then beat until the mixture is thick and forms stiff peaks — electric beaters make light work of this. Fill the biscuits with the cream. Makes about 25.

lamingtons

185 g (1 1/2 cups) self-raising flour
4 tbs cornflour (cornstarch)
175 g (6 oz) unsalted butter, softened
250 g (1 cup) caster (superfine) sugar
2 tsp natural vanilla extract
3 eggs, lightly beaten
125 ml (1/2 cup) milk

For the icing:
500 g (4 cups) icing (confectioners') sugar
4 tbs cocoa powder
30 g (1 oz) unsalted butter, melted
170 ml (2/3 cup) milk
270 g (3 cups) desiccated coconut

Sift the flour and cornflour into a large bowl. Add the butter, sugar, vanilla extract, eggs and milk. Start with the beaters on low speed until the ingredients are just moist, then whir at high speed until fluffy and smooth. Pour it into a lined, shallow 23 cm (9 inch) square cake tin and smooth the surface. Bake in a 180°C (350°F/Gas 4) oven for 50 minutes until ready (when a skewer comes out clean). Leave in the tin for a few minutes then cool on a wire rack. Get a knife (serrated is best) and trim the top of the cake flat. Now trim the sides and cut the cake into 16 squares.

To make the icing, sift the icing sugar and cocoa into a heatproof bowl and add the butter and milk. Balance the bowl over a saucepan of simmering water and keep stirring until smooth and glossy, then take it off the heat. Sprinkle a third of the coconut on a sheet of baking paper. The aim now is to coat the cake with icing, then coconut — it's easiest if you spear the cake squares with two forks and let the chocolate drain off before you roll it in the coconut. Keep going, adding the extra coconut when you need it — it will stay clean for longer if you add it bit by bit. Makes 16.

A lamington is as Australian as mom's apple pie is American, and just as ubiquitous. You'll find the sponge cake easier to handle if it's left for one day before cutting.

An angel food cake needs to be cooked in a tube pan — a round, deep tin with a hollow tube in the centre — or a bundt pan, a tin of similar proportions with fluted sides.

angel food cake

125 g (1 cup) self-raising flour
375 g (1½ cups) caster (superfine) sugar
12 egg whites
1½ tsp cream of tartar
½ tsp natural vanilla extract
¼ tsp almond extract
icing (confectioners') sugar
sliced fresh fruit

Sift the flour and 185 g (¾ cup) sugar together four times to add lots of air to the flour and help the cake become light as air.

Beat the egg whites with the cream of tartar and ¼ teaspoon salt until you have a mound of stiff peaks. Next, beat in the remaining sugar, a tablespoon at a time until you have a thick, glossy mixture. Now fold in the vanilla and almond extracts. Sift a quarter of the flour and sugar mixture onto the egg white and, using a spatula, gradually fold in. Repeat with the remaining flour and sugar.

Spoon the mixture into the angel food tin and bake in a 180°C (350°F/Gas 4) oven for 35–40 minutes, or until puffed and golden, and a skewer inserted in the centre comes out clean. Turn upside-down on a wire rack and leave in the tin until cool. Gently shake to remove the cake. Lightly dust with icing sugar and serve with fruit.
Serves 8.

Angel food cake can be served with fresh fruit and whipped cream as a dessert cake.

chocolate swiss roll

3 eggs
125 g (1/2 cup) caster (superfine) sugar
3 tbs plain (all-purpose) flour
2 tbs cocoa powder
250 ml (1 cup) whipping cream
1 tbs icing (confectioners') sugar, plus extra
1/2 tsp natural vanilla extract

Lightly grease a swiss roll tin, then line it with baking paper, letting the paper hang over the long sides. Beat the eggs and 4 tablespoons caster sugar in a small bowl until thick and creamy — electric beaters make this a cinch. Fold in the combined sifted flour and cocoa.

Spread the mixture into the tin and smooth the surface. Bake in a 200°C (400°F/Gas 6) oven until just set — it will only need 10 minutes. While the cake is cooking, lay a clean tea towel on a bench, cover with baking paper and sprinkle with the remaining caster sugar. As soon as the cake is cooked, turn it out onto the sugar. Roll the cake up from the short side, rolling the paper inside the roll and using the tea towel as a guide. Stand the rolled cake on a wire rack for 5 minutes, then carefully unroll and let the cake cool to room temperature. Neaten the ends with a knife.

Now for the filling: beat the cream, icing sugar and vanilla into stiff peaks, then spread over the cooled cake, leaving a thin border. Using the paper as a guide, re-roll the cake. Sit the roll, seam-side down, on a tray in the fridge for 30 minutes. Dust with icing sugar, then serve. Serves 6.

A scrumptious variation of the jam roll that's just as moist and just as tempting with its neat chocolate and cream spiral.

index

Alaska, Baked, 210

almonds, Trout with, 91

Angel food cake, 249

Angels and devils on horseback, 11

Apricot chicken, 63

asparagus soup, Cream of, 44

Baked Alaska, 210

Baked cheesecake, 233

Bakewell slice, 238

Banana fritters, 209

Barbecued honey chicken wings, 36

bean burrito bake, Beef and kidney, 72

beef

   and kidney bean burrito bake, 72

   Boeuf Bourguignon, 127

carbonnade, 124

Carpaccio, 48

Carpetbag steak, 95

Chateaubriand, 100

Chilli con carne, 103

Fajitas, 80

Moussaka, 115

pot roast, 128

Pepper steak, 76

Peppered beef fillet with béarnaise sauce, 104

Steak Diane, 68

Steak tartare, 88

Steak with green peppercorn sauce, 84

stroganoff, 139

Teppanyaki, 67

Tournedos rossini, 96

Tournedos sautés chasseur, 144

wellington, 147

Black forest gateau, 202

Boeuf Bourguignon, 127

bolognese, Spaghetti, 64

Brandy snaps, 245

Bread and butter pudding, 222

cacciatore, Chicken, 135

cakes

   Angel food, 249

   Baked cheesecake, 233

   Black forest gateau, 202

   Chocolate Swiss roll, 250

   Pineapple upside-down cake, 230

   Sachertorte, 229

calamari with tartare sauce, Fried, 32

capsicums with tomato sauce, Stuffed, 187

Caramel slice, 241

carbonnade, Beef, 124

Carpaccio, 48

Carpetbag steak, 95

carrots, Vichy, 162

Cauliflower cheese, 169

Chateaubriand, 100

cheese

   Cauliflower, 169

   fondue, 83

   Macaroni, 179

   soufflé, 180

   straws, 16

chicken

   Apricot, 63

   Country-fried, 107

   cacciatore, 135

   Coq au vin, 140

   cordon bleu, 79

   Kiev, 99

   liver pâté, 35

   teriyaki, 112

   wings, Barbecued honey, 36

Chilli con carne, 103

Chillies rellenos, 27

chocolate

   fondue, 225

   mousse, Creamy, 197

   soufflé, Hot, 214

   Swiss roll, 250

   truffles, Rich, 242

Coconut jam slice, 234

Coleslaw, 157

Coq au vin, 140

Coulibiac, 188

cordon bleu, Chicken, 79

cordon bleu, Veal, 92

Country-fried chicken, 107

Crème brûlée, 218

Crêpes suzette, 198

Croquettes, 158

date pudding, Sticky, 06

Dauphinoise, 170

devils on horseback, Angels and, 11

Duchess potatoes, 165

Duck a l'orange, 116

eggs, Scotch quail, 31

Fajitas, 80

Fettucine carbonara, 132

Fish pie, 75

flan, Fruit, 201

fondue, Cheese, 83

fondue, Chocolate, 225

French onion soup, 52

fritters, Banana, 209

Fruit flan, 201

Garlic prawns, 56

guacamole, Munchy potato skins with, 161

Gazpacho, 47

Glazed ham, 148

goulash, Veal, 143

ham, Glazed, 148

Hush puppies, 28

kedgeree, Lightly spiced, 176

Key lime pie, 205

Kiev, Chicken, 99

koftas with cooling yoghurt dip, Spicy, 20

Lamingtons, 246
Lasagne, 71
Lemon meringue pie, 221
loaf, Meat, 108
Lobster mornay, 131

Macaroni cheese, 179
Meat loaf, 108
meatballs, Spaghetti with, 120
minestrone, Hearty, 191
mornay, Lobster, 131
mornay, Tuna, 119
Moussaka, 115
mousse, Creamy chocolate, 197

nachos, Party, 184

Onion bhajis with spicy sauce, 19

parmigiana, Veal, 111
parsley sauce, Silverside with, 123

pasta
    Fettucine carbonara, 132
    Lasagne, 71
    Macaroni cheese, 179
    Spaghetti bolognese, 64
    Spaghetti with meatballs, 120
pâté, Chicken liver, 35
pâté, Smoked trout, 12
Pepper steak, 76
Peppered beef fillet with béarnaise sauce, 104
pies
    Fish, 75
    Key lime, 205
    Lemon meringue, 221
    Shepherd's, 136
Pineapple upside-down cake, 230
Porcupine balls, 23
pot roast, Beef, 128
potato
    Croquettes, 158
    Dauphinoise, 170
    Duchess potatoes, 165
    Rosti, 166

salad, 153
skins with guacamole, Munchy, 161
Sautéed, 154
Prawn and mango salad, 59
Prawn cocktail, 43
prawns, Garlic, 56
pudding, Bread and butter, 222
pudding, Sticky date, 206
pumpkin soup, Roast, 51
puppies, Hush, 28

Quiche Lorraine, 183

rolls, Classic sausage, 175
rolls, Spring, 39
Rosti, 166

Sachertorte, 229
salads
    Coleslaw, 157
    Potato, 153
    Prawn and mango, 59
sausage rolls, Classic, 175
Scotch quail eggs, 31

Shepherd's pie, 136

Silverside with parsley sauce, 123

slices

Bakewell, 238

Caramel, 241

Coconut jam, 234

White Christmas, 237

Smoked trout pâté, 12

snaps, Brandy, 245

soufflé, Cheese, 180

soufflé, Hot chocolate, 214

soups

Cream of asparagus, 44

French onion, 52

Gazpacho, 47

minestrone, Hearty, 191

Roast pumpkin, 51

Vichyssoise, 55

Spaghetti bolognese, 64

Spaghetti with meatballs, 120

spicy sauce, Onion bhajis with, 19

Spring rolls, 39

steaks

Carpetbag, 95

Pepper steak, 76

Steak Diane, 68

Steak tartare, 88

Steak with green peppercorn sauce, 84

Sticky date pudding, 206

straws, Cheese, 16

stroganoff, Beef, 139

Stuffed capsicums with tomato sauce, 187

Swiss roll, Chocolate, 250

Taramasalata, 15

tartare sauce, Fried calamari with, 32

Teppanyaki, 67

teriyaki, Chicken, 112

Tiramisu, 217

tomato sauce, Stuffed capsicums with, 187

Tournedos rossini, 96

Tournedos sautés chasseur, 144

Trifle, 213

Trout with almonds, 91

truffles, Rich chocolate, 242

Tuna mornay, 119

veal

cordon bleu, 92

goulash, 143

parmigiana, 111

Wiener schnitzel, 87

Vichy carrots, 162

Vichyssoise, 55

wellington, Beef, 147

Welsh rarebit, 192

White Christmas, 237

whitebait, Fried, 24

Wiener schnitzel, 87

yoghurt dip, Spicy koftas with cooling, 20